JOURNEYS

Reader's Notebook
Volume 1

Grade 3

Houghton Mifflin Harcourt

Printed in the U.S.A.

ISBN 978-0-544-59263-6

25 26 27 28 29 0304 26 25 24 23 22

4500849469   B C D E F G

Contents

Words with Short Vowels

**Read each word. Then find and circle it in the Word Find.
Words can go across or down.**

gentle	empty	visit	lily
softly	glance	puppy	tumble

```
s  o  v  t  l  y  u  s  o
p  v  i  s  i  t  s  o  y
u  i  l  o  g  u  f  f  s
p  s  y  f  e  m  p  t  y
p  g  l  a  n  c  e  l  t
y  l  i  e  t  u  m  y  o
p  u  l  m  l  i  l  e  s
t  u  y  p  e  m  y  l  y
b  m  u  t  u  m  b  l  e
```

Write each word in the correct place in the chart below.

Words with Short Vowels

a	e	i	o	u

The Subject of a Simple Sentence

- A sentence is a group of words that tells a complete thought. The **subject** of a simple sentence tells whom or what the sentence is about.

- The subject usually comes at the beginning of the sentence. The subject can be one word or more than one word. The **complete subject** includes all the words in the subject.

    The weekend is a special time.

    My family enjoys the holidays.

Thinking Question
Whom or what is the sentence about?

Write the complete subject of each simple sentence.

1. Saturday is a fun day. _____

2. All my friends get together in the park. _____

3. Baseball teams play on the fields. _____

4. My father coaches the teams. _____

5. My mother watches all the games. _____

6. Our neighbors bring lots of food. _____

7. We cook outside until it is dark. _____

8. The kids sleep on a blanket. _____

9. Grandma and Grandpa tell stories. _____

10. Many of our teachers join us. _____

Name _____ Date _____

Lesson 1
READER'S NOTEBOOK

A Fine, Fine School
Grammar:
Simple Sentences

The Predicate of a Simple Sentence

- Every simple sentence has two parts—the subject and the predicate.

- The **predicate** is the part of a sentence that tells what the subject does or is.

- The predicate can be one word or more than one word. The **complete predicate** includes all the words in the predicate.

  I lie beside the river.

  My body relaxes in the sun.

Thinking Question
Which word or words in the sentence tell what the subject does or is?

Write each sentence. Then underline the complete predicate.

1. Relaxing is not as easy as it looks.

_____

2. I like to watch the clouds above me.

_____

3. Gerry enjoys floating in the pool.

_____

4. Ernie sits on the back steps with his dog.

_____

5. My cousins swing in tires hung from ropes.

_____

Spelling Word Sort

Write each Basic Word under the correct heading.
One word will go under two different headings.

Short *a*	Short *e*
_____	_____
_____	_____
_____	_____

Short *i*	Short *o*
_____	_____
_____	_____
_____	_____
_____	**Short *u***
_____	_____
_____	_____
_____	_____

Spelling Words

Basic
1. crop
2. plan
3. thing
4. smell
5. shut
6. sticky
7. spent
8. lunch
9. pumpkin
10. clock
11. gift
12. class
13. skip
14. swing

Review
next
hug

Challenge
hospital
fantastic

Review: Add the Review Words to your Word Sort.

Challenge: Which Challenge Word has short vowels *o* and *i*?

_____

Focus Trait: Elaboration

Exact Words

Without Exact Words	With Exact Words
Mr. Brown lived in a big house.	Mr. Brown lived in the enormous, old green mansion on the hill, behind Taft Middle School.

A. Read the sentence that does not use exact words. Then choose words and add details to make the description more exact.

Without Exact Words	With Exact Words
1. Every day I go to school.	Every _____ I _____ to _____.

B. Read each sentence that does not use exact words. Then look at the illustration on pages 26–27 of *A Fine, Fine School*. **Rewrite the sentence using exact words.**

Pair/Share   Work with a partner to brainstorm exact words to use.

Without Exact Words	With Exact Words
2. The children are staying busy.	
3. Mr. Keene is making a face.	
4. The children are using their lockers.	

Words with the VCCV Pattern

Write a word from the box to complete each sentence in
the story.

basket	happened	suddenly
chipmunk	princess	garden
rabbit	puppet	trumpet
galloped		

1. The blaring _____ announced the show
   would soon begin.

2. Children sat in front of a little stage in the _____.

3. Everyone was excited to see the _____
   show.

4. A furry _____ was the first puppet
   onstage.

5. Next came a little _____ puppet.

6. What _____ next was a surprise.

7. The rabbit told the chipmunk she was really a beautiful

   _____.

8. The chipmunk gave the rabbit a _____ of flowers.

9. The rabbit _____ disappeared, and a
   beautiful princess stood in her place.

10. The princess and the chipmunk _____ away on
    a horse.

Reader's Guide

A Fine, Fine School

The Fine, Fine School Times

Tillie is writing an article for the school newspaper, *The Fine, Fine School Times*. Her article will tell the real story. Use the text and illustrations to help her write the article.

Read pages 20–23. How do the students and teachers feel about going to school on the weekends and during the summer?

Mr. Keene just announced school will be open every single day of the year. I talked to some students and teachers. The students feel that _____

_____

The teachers are worried that they might _____

_____

Mr. Keene has a different opinion. He thinks that the teachers and students will love coming to school every day because _____

_____

That's all the news for now!

Read pages 30–33. Now Mr. Keene has changed his mind about keeping school open every day. Tillie has written another article to share the news.

The big news in school today is that school will be closed on weekends and during the summer. Mr. Keene said that the main reason for the change was

_____

_____

I talked to some students about the change. One student told me that she liked the days off because

_____

_____

Another student told me that now when he was not in school he could learn other things, like

_____

The teachers and students are all pleased with Mr. Keene's decision. That is all the news for now from *The Fine, Fine School Times.*

Name _____ Date _____

Lesson 1
READER'S NOTEBOOK

A Fine, Fine School
Grammar:
Simple Sentences

Sentence Fragments

Write the complete subject of each simple sentence.
Then underline the complete predicate.

1. Ira loves to read books in summer. _____

2. Gina helps her dad all summer. _____

3. Michaela rides her bike. _____

4. Wanda and Jane planted a garden. _____

5. The kids on Roy's block play baseball. _____

Write a complete simple sentence for each sentence fragment.

6. Tera and her swim team.

   _____

7. Has games all summer.

   _____

8. Have frozen treats.

   _____

9. My friend.

   _____

10. In the car.

   _____

9

Name _____ Date _____

Short Vowels

Write a Basic Word to finish the second sentence in each pair of sentences.

1. Water is wet.

   Glue is _____.

2. You eat breakfast in the morning.

   You eat _____ at noon.

3. You use a ruler to measure length.

   You use a _____ to measure time.

4. You see with your eyes.

   You _____ with your nose.

5. A writer writes a book.

   A farmer plants a _____.

6. You can earn money by doing a job.

   When your money is gone, it is _____.

7. Watermelons are seen in summer.

   _____ are seen in fall.

8. A wolf is part of a pack.

   A student is part of a _____.

9. A horse learns to prance.

   A child learns to _____.

10. Before you enter, you must open a door.

    When you leave, you _____ the door.

Challenge: Make up a pair of sentences similar to the ones above. Use a Challenge Word as the answer.

Spelling Words

Basic
1. crop
2. plan
3. thing
4. smell
5. shut
6. sticky
7. spent
8. lunch
9. pumpkin
10. clock
11. gift
12. class
13. skip
14. swing

Review
next
hug

Challenge
hospital
fantastic

Context Clues

**Read the sentence. Write the meaning of the underlined word
as it is used in the sentence. Use a dictionary if you need help.**

1. One <u>fine</u> day when the weather was nice, our family went on a picnic.

_____

2. We ate sandwiches and tried a new <u>kind</u> of juice drink.

_____

3. We plan to take another <u>trip</u> to the park soon.

_____

4. Elena was <u>fatigued</u> after the long, busy day.

_____

5. The <u>immense</u> sign blocked our view of the building.

_____

6. The winter day is too <u>frigid</u> to go outdoors.

_____

7. Jeffrey was so surprised at what he saw, he couldn't stop <u>gaping</u>.

_____

8. The detective had a <u>crucial</u> piece of information about the theft.

_____

Capitalization and Punctuation

- Correct **capitalization** includes capitalizing the first letter of sentences.
- Every sentence has end **punctuation**, such as a period.

    My pencil needs to be sharpened.

    Now my writing will be easy to read.

Write each sentence using correct capitalization and punctuation.

1. our school principal visited our class today

_____

2. all students will take the test next week

_____

3. the math teacher surprised all of us

_____

4. that is my favorite book

_____

5. today is a holiday

_____

6. i saw Mr. Clarke yesterday

_____

Proofreading for Spelling

Read the following invitation. Find and circle the misspelled words.

Spelling Words

Basic

1. crop
2. plan
3. thing
4. smell
5. shut
6. sticky
7. spent
8. lunch
9. pumpkin
10. clock
11. gift
12. class
13. skip
14. swing

Review

next

hug

Challenge

hospital

fantastic

You're Invited!

Please plen to attend Mr. Hay's cless next Monday.

We have spint three weeks learning about autumn. We want to share some of the thangs we learned with you.

We will begin when the cluck strikes ten. We will shet the doors at that time. We will teach you about some crups farmers grow in our area in the fall. Then we will discuss interesting facts about the sun and Earth at this time of year. Finally, we will eat. You will be hungry from the delicious smill of pompken pie! It will be our gaft to you.

Write the misspelled words correctly on the lines below.

1. _____   6. _____

2. _____   7. _____

3. _____   8. _____

4. _____   9. _____

5. _____   10. _____

Connect to Writing

Sometimes a sentence does not include a complete thought. It is a **fragment**. Correct fragments by adding the missing subject or predicate. This will make your writing easier to understand.

Fragments	Complete Simple Sentences
Taught our cat to fetch. Raul taught.	Raul taught our cat to fetch.
My sister. Showed the puppy tricks.	My sister showed the puppy tricks.

Correct the fragments by combining the subjects and predicates to form complete simple sentences. Write the sentence on the line.

1. Our dog. Loves bones.

_____

2. Grandpa a trick. Taught him a trick.

_____

3. Dogs attention. Love attention.

_____

4. Danny taught. Our dog to sit.

_____

5. The dog to come. Begged us to come.

_____

Words with Long Vowels

Read each clue. Write two rhyming words from the
Word Bank to answer the clue.

base	rage	globe	joke
home	shade	skate	lime
broke	chase	plate	tone
robe	chrome	slime	phone
cage	shake	snake	trade

1. If you chase your friend around the bases on a field, you

play a game of _____ _____.

2. If a joke wasn't funny, the _____ _____.

3. If a lime rots, you will have _____ _____.

4. A snake that is cold does a _____ _____.

5. An angry bird in a cage may get _____ _____.

6. If you put paper plates under your feet, you can go for a _____

_____.

7. If you put on a bathrobe with a round map of the world on it, you are

wearing a _____ _____.

8. If you switch shady spots, you do a _____ _____.

9. When you pick up a telephone, you hear a sound called a

_____ _____.

10. A shiny, silver house is a _____ _____.

Name _____ Date _____

Lesson 2
READER'S NOTEBOOK

The Trial of
Cardigan Jones
Grammar:
Kinds of Sentences

Statements and Questions

- Every sentence begins with a capital letter. There are four kinds of sentences. Statements and questions are two of them.

- A sentence that tells something is a **statement**. It ends with a period. It is also called a **declarative** sentence.

- A sentence that asks something is a **question**. It ends with a question mark. It is also called an **interrogative** sentence.

Thinking Question
Is the sentence a statement or a question, and how do I know?

Statement/Declarative
I wear comfortable clothes.

Question/Interrogative
What do you like to wear?

Write *statement* if the sentence tells something. Write *question* if the sentence asks something.

1. I wear old shirts around the house. _____

2. Why don't you go and change your clothes? _____

3. Who is coming to visit? _____

4. I dress up for company. _____

5. Why do my old clothes feel so good? _____

6. Old cotton shirts are very soft. _____

7. A new dress can feel strange. _____

8. My pet moves around the house. _____

Name _____ Date _____

Lesson 2
READER'S NOTEBOOK

**The Trial of
Cardigan Jones**
Grammar:
Kinds of Sentences

Commands and Exclamations

- Two kinds of sentences are statements and questions. Two other kinds of sentences are **commands** and **exclamations**.

- A **command** is a sentence that tells someone to do something. It ends with a period. It is also called an **imperative** sentence.

- An **exclamation** is a sentence that shows strong feeling, such as excitement, surprise, or fear. It ends with an exclamation point. It is also called an **exclamatory** sentence.

- All kinds of sentences should begin with a capital letter and end with proper punctuation.

Command/Imperative	Get a chair, please.
Exclamation/Exclamatory	I'm excited!

Thinking Question
Is the sentence a command or an exclamation, and what punctuation does it end with?

Write *command* if the sentence tells someone to do something.
Write *exclamation* if the sentence shows strong feeling.

1. That is the funniest joke! _____

2. Tell another joke. _____

3. I am so happy! _____

4. Bring everyone in to hear these. _____

5. How my sides hurt from laughing! _____

6. Pull out those chairs and sit down. _____

7. Please repeat that joke. _____

**The Trial of
Cardigan Jones**
Spelling:
VC*e* Spellings

Spelling Word Sort

Write each Basic Word under the correct heading.

Long *a*	Long *i*
1. _____	4. _____
2. _____	5. _____
3. _____	6. _____
	7. _____
	8. _____

Long *o*	Long *u*
9. _____	12. _____
10. _____	13. _____
11. _____	14. _____

Review: What long vowel sound does the Review Word *these*

have? _____ What long vowel sound does the

Review Word *those* have? _____

Challenge: In which column do the two Challenge Words

belong? _____

Spelling Words

Basic
1. spoke
2. mile
3. save
4. excuse
5. cone
6. invite
7. cube
8. price
9. erase
10. ripe
11. broke
12. flame
13. life
14. rule

Review
these
those

Challenge
surprise
decide

Focus Trait: Conventions
Sentence Types

Without a Variety of Sentence Types	With a Variety of Sentence Types
The milkman told the judge what he saw.	"Judge, I'm sure I saw the moose tiptoe up to the window. He put his face right into the pie!" said the milkman.

A. Read the sentence below. Rewrite it as a paragraph using a variety of sentence types.

Without a Variety of Sentence Types	With a Variety of Sentence Types
1. The moose was clumsy.	

B. Read each sentence below. Rewrite the sentences, adding a variety of sentence types that will bring your story to life for the reader.

Pair/Share Work with a partner to add a variety of sentence types.

Without a Variety of Sentence Types	With a Variety of Sentence Types
2. Page 54: Mrs. Brown didn't know what happened to her pie.	
3. Page 66: The judge found the missing pie.	

Words with the VC*e* Pattern

Read each word. Draw a line to match the word to its meaning.

Column 1	Column 2
1. awake	a. clothes worn to make somebody look like somebody or something else
2. costume	b. to free oneself or get away from
3. divide	c. to bring things together
4. escape	d. an error
5. exercise	e. not asleep
6. microphone	f. a paved path where people can walk alongside a street
7. mistake	g. to separate
8. refuse	h. to say no
9. sidewalk	i. to work out or do a physical activity
10. unite	j. a device to make someone's voice louder

Write each word from Column 1 in the correct place in the chart below. Look at the part of the word with the VC*e* pattern.

Long *a*	Long *i*	Long *o*	Long *u*

Name _____ Date _____

Lesson 2
READER'S NOTEBOOK

The Trial of
Cardigan Jones
Independent Reading

Reader's Guide

The Trial of Cardigan Jones

Questions for the Milkman

What would you say if you were the milkman? Right now, the judge is asking you questions about Cardigan Jones. Use the text and illustrations to explain exactly what you saw that day.

What were you doing right before Mrs. Brown's pie was stolen?

Read page 53.

_____

_____

Now tell me exactly what you saw when you looked out of your truck.

_____

_____

_____

In your own words, tell me why you think Cardigan Jones stole the pie.

Read pages 60–61.

_____

_____

Read page 62.

What have you observed about Cardigan Jones in this courtroom?

_____

_____

Read page 67.

So now we know what really happened to the pie. Tell me, Milkman, how do you feel?

_____

_____

Read page 69.

How would you describe Cardigan Jones now that you know him better?

_____

_____

Name _____ Date _____

Lesson 2
READER'S NOTEBOOK

The Trial of
Cardigan Jones
Grammar:
Kinds of Sentences

Statements, Questions, Commands, and Exclamations

Write *statement* if the sentence tells something. Write *question* if the sentence asks something.

1. I like basketball. _____

2. I would not want to climb a mountain. _____

3. Where do you row your boat? _____

4. Do you like to play tennis? _____

5. What do you know about judo? _____

Write *command* if the sentence tells someone to do something.
Write *exclamation* if the sentence shows strong feeling.

6. Pick up the tennis racket. _____

7. Tennis is a great sport! _____

8. Please join me in a game. _____

9. Ask him to play tennis with us. _____

10. I will not ask him! _____

Name _____   Date _____

VC*e* Spellings

Write the Basic Word that belongs in each group.

1. sphere, pyramid, _____,

   _____

2. fire, smoke, _____

3. inch, yard, _____

4. ask, call, _____

5. ready, full-grown, _____

6. whispered, yelled, _____

7. ___ _____

8. change, wipe away, _____

9. rescue, free, _____

10. amount, cost, _____

Challenge: Which Challenge Word belongs in a group called
Things That Are Unexpected? _____

Spelling Words

Basic
1. spoke
2. mile
3. save
4. excuse
5. cone
6. invite
7. cube
8. price
9. erase
10. ripe
11. broke
12. name
13. life
14. rule

Review
these
those

Challenge
surprise
decide

Dictionary/Glossary

Read each word. Find each word in a dictionary or glossary.
Complete the chart.

Word	Part(s) of Speech	Word with Endings
1. gavel		
2. pilfer		
3. declare		
4. testify		
5. fine		

Now write one sentence of your own that could be an example
sentence for one meaning of each word.

1. _____

2. _____

3. _____

4. _____

5. _____

Name _____ Date _____

Lesson 2
READER'S NOTEBOOK

The Trial of Cardigan Jones
Grammar:
Spiral Review

Writing Subjects and Predicates

- The **subject** of a sentence tells whom or what the sentence is about. The main word in a sentence is often a **noun**. It is called the **simple subject**.
- The **predicate** of a sentence tells what the subject is or was ~~or what the subject does or did~~. The main word in the predicate is a **verb**. It is called the **simple predicate**.

The complete subject of each sentence is underlined. Write the simple subject.

1. The room for the dance was large. _____

2. The band's first song had a fast tempo. _____

3. The twins said they would dance to every song. _____

4. The girl in the yellow dress danced happily. _____

The complete predicate of each sentence is underlined. Write the simple predicate.

5. The teachers put drinks and snacks on the tables. _____

6. I looked for my cousin on the dance floor. _____

7. Everyone danced to the last song. _____

8. The tired dancers walked home happy. _____

Proofreading for Spelling

**The Trial of
Cardigan Jones**
Spelling:
VC*e* Spellings

Read the following passage. Find and circle the misspelled words.

> Do you sometimes wish there was no such thing as a roole? Let's think about how lief would be different without rules. You may surpris yourself and be thankful for rules!
>
> Let's say you have an ice cream con. I see it and decid I want it. I take your ice cream. I do not say excoose me. I eat it all, even though you paid the prise for it.
>
> Thos actions would make you mad, wouldn't they? But since there are no rules, the only thing I brok was your pride. I did not break a rule.
>
> Rules saav us from situations like these. Rules help us all get along.

Write the misspelled words correctly on the lines below.

1. _____   6. _____

2. _____   7. _____

3. _____   8. _____

4. _____   9. _____

5. _____   10. _____

Spelling Words

Basic
1. spoke
2. mile
3. save
4. excuse
5. cone
6. invite
7. cube
8. price
9. erase
10. ripe
11. broke
12. flame
13. life
14. rule

Review
these
those

Challenge
surprise
decide

Name _____   Date _____

Lesson 2
READER'S NOTEBOOK

The Trial of
Cardigan Jones
Grammar:
Connect to Writing

Connect to Writing

Sentences can be statements, questions, commands, or exclamations. Using all four kinds of sentences in a paragraph makes writing more lively and varied.

Paragraph with One Kind of Sentence	Paragraph with Four Kinds of Sentences
Rowing a boat can be lots of fun. You should try it. You find a boat. You will laugh a lot.	Rowing a boat can be lots of fun. Why don't you try it? Find a boat. You will not stop laughing!

Change each sentence to another type of sentence. The word in parentheses tells you the type of sentence to write. Write the new sentence on the line.

1. We won the boat race. (exclamation)

_____

2. Do you row the boats there? (statement)

_____

3. Can we put this boat in the water? (command)

_____

4. We should watch the boat race. (question)

_____

5. Will you let me ride in the boat? (statement)

_____

Common Vowel Pairs
ai, ay, ee, ea

Write the word from the Word Bank that best completes each sentence.

always	easel	stain	steam
bait	greedy	players	sweeten
breeze	rain	queen	trail
chain	layers	seasons	

1. Of all the _____, fall is my favorite.

2. When you boil water, the _____ you see is the water vapor.

3. Take your umbrella because it will _____.

4. The door is secured with a lock and strong _____.

5. I knew it was the _____ because of her crown.

6. The hikers walked along the marked _____.

7. The artist paints at his _____.

8. To be safe, I _____ look both ways at a stop sign.

9. I will use honey to _____ the iced tea.

10. The cake has three different _____.

11. The spilled juice left a _____ on the carpet.

12. On a hot day, a _____ is welcome.

13. Remember to take the _____ with you when you go fishing.

14. Four _____ can play the game at the same time.

15. If you do not share, people may think you are _____.

Destiny's Gift
Grammar:
Compound Sentences

Simple and Compound Sentences

- A **simple sentence** tells a complete thought.
- A **compound sentence** is made up of two simple sentences joined by the word *and*, *but*, *or*, or *so*.

    We stood in the front yard. Our neighbors stayed indoors.

    We stood in the front yard, but our neighbors stayed indoors.

Thinking Question
Does the sentence tell one complete thought, or does it tell two complete thoughts?

**Determine whether each sentence is simple or compound.
Write *simple* or *compound* on the line.**

1. Young students and their friends met at the bookstore.

   _____

2. The children handed out flyers, and their parents carried

   signs. _____

3. A large group of people shouted, but they were not angry.

   _____

4. They shouted to get people to come to the bookstore.

   _____

5. Many old customers came, and some customers gave

   speeches. _____

6. People could buy books, or they could donate money.

   _____

Coordinating Conjunctions

Destiny's Gift
Grammar:
Compound Sentences

- A **compound sentence** is made up of two simple sentences joined by a conjunction.
- The words *and*, *but*, *or*, and *so* are **conjunctions**. A comma comes before the conjunction.

    And joins two similar ideas.

    But joins two different ideas.

    Or joins two possible ideas.

    So shows that the second idea happens because of the first.

Thinking Question
Which kinds of ideas are being joined into one sentence?

Write the conjunction that best joins the simple sentences. Then write the compound sentence.

1. Dora called Lisa. She called Erin.

   _____

   _____

2. Erin was at home. Lisa was not at home.

   _____

   _____

3. Erin did not have plans. She could visit Dora.

   _____

   _____

4. Erin could bring a game. She could bring a movie.

   _____

   _____

Destiny's Gift
Spelling:
Long a and Long e Spellings

Spelling Word Sort

Write each Basic Word under the correct heading.

Long *a* Spelled *ay*	Long *a* Spelled *ai*
_____	_____
_____	_____
_____	_____
_____	_____
_____	_____

Long *e* Spelled *ee*	Long *e* Spelled *ea*
_____	_____
_____	_____
_____	_____
_____	_____
_____	_____

Review: Add the Review Words to your Word Sort.

Challenge: Add the Challenge Words to your Word Sort.

Spelling Words

Basic
1. lay
2. real
3. trail
4. sweet
5. today
6. dream
7. seem
8. tea
9. treat
10. afraid
11. leave
12. bait
13. cheer
14. speed

Review
paint
please

Challenge
yesterday
explain

Focus Trait: Development
Express Thoughts and Feelings

These thoughts and feelings...	...help you understand this.
Destiny remembers how much she enjoyed talking with writers. She describes how they shared her love of words.	They show how Destiny feels about talking to authors, and they explain why Destiny wants to become a writer.

A. Read the event from *Destiny's Gift*. Underline the words that show Destiny's thoughts and feelings. Then explain what they help you understand about Destiny.

These thoughts and feelings...	...help you understand this.
1. Destiny can't stop crying after she finds out about Mrs. Wade's store.	

B. Read each sentence that tells an event from *Destiny's Gift*. Look at the page listed. Write a sentence that tells about Destiny's or Mrs. Wade's thoughts and feelings.

Pair/Share   Work with a partner before you write.

Event	Sentence with Thoughts and Feelings
2. Page 88: Destiny says she likes Mrs. Wade's bookstore.	
3. Page 104: Destiny writes something for Mrs. Wade.	

Destiny's Gift
Phonics:
Cumulative Review

Name _____ Date _____

Cumulative Review

Read the grocery list. Write each item in the chart below.

Grocery List

artichokes	grapes	peaches
beans	lemonade	peanuts
beef	limes	pineapple
cheese	grains	prunes
coffee	oatmeal	crayfish

Long a		Long e		Long i spelled VCe	Long o spelled VCe	Long u spelled VCe
VCe		VCe				
ai		ee				
ay		ea				

Write a recipe on another sheet of paper. Use at least three
words on the list. You can use other ingredients, too.

Run-On Sentences

- Two or more simple sentences that run together are called **run-on** sentences.
- A run-on sentence may be corrected by forming a **compound sentence**. The conjunctions *and*, *but*, *or*, and *so* are used to form compound sentences.

Thinking Question
Can I use a conjunction to join these sentences and form a compound sentence?

Rita does not like moose Gwen does.
Rita does not like moose, but Gwen does.

Correct each run-on sentence by forming a compound sentence. Write the conjunction and then write the compound sentence.

1. Moose are a kind of deer they are part of the deer family.

_____

_____

2. Adult males have large antlers female moose do not.

_____

_____

3. Moose are good swimmers they are fast runners.

_____

_____

4. The moose might bellow the moose might grunt.

_____

_____

Long *a* and Long *e* Spellings

Write a Basic Word to answer each clue. Then use letters in the word to answer the second clue. The letters may not be in the correct order.

Spelling Words

Basic
1. lay
2. real
3. trail
4. sweet
5. today
6. dream
7. seem
8. tea
9. treat
10. afraid
11. leave
12. bait
13. screen
14. speed

Review
paint
please

Challenge
yesterday
explain

1. what helps you catch fish ___ ___ ___ ___

   what you swing in baseball ___ ___ ___

2. how fast you go ___ ___ ___ ___ ___

   not shallow ___ ___ ___ ___

3. something you do when you sleep ___ ___ ___ ___ ___

   what you do with a book ___ ___ ___ ___

4. candy has this taste ___ ___ ___ ___ ___

   a direction on a map ___ ___ ___ ___

5. a reward for a good dog ___ ___ ___ ___ ___

   what you do with food ___ ___ ___

6. to go away ___ ___ ___ ___ ___

   a snake-like fish ___ ___ ___

7. to look or appear to be true ___ ___ ___ ___

   your eyes do this for you ___ ___ ___

8. something you might walk on in the woods ___ ___ ___ ___ ___

   a rodent with a long tail ___ ___ ___

Antonyms

lower	all	left
after	take	last

Read each word below. Write the antonym from the box above.
Then write a sentence using both words.

1. none _____

_____

2. first _____

_____

3. raise _____

_____

4. right _____

_____

5. before _____

_____

6. give _____

_____

Name _____ Date _____

Lesson 3
READER'S NOTEBOOK

Destiny's Gift
Grammar:
Spiral Review

Kinds of Sentences

> - There are four kinds of sentences.
>
>   Mom is home. **Declarative** (statement)
>
>   Did you study? **Interrogative** (question)
>
>   Pick up that mess. **Imperative** (command)
>
>   What a great job! **Exclamatory** (exclamation)

Write _statement_ if the sentence tells something. Write _question_ if the sentence asks something.

1. John brought his lunch to the picnic. _____

2. Are you going to the picnic? _____

3. Will you bring a friend? _____

Write _command_ if the sentence tells someone to do something. Write _exclamation_ if the sentence shows strong feeling.

4. The picnic is really going to be fun! _____

5. Hand me that plate. _____

6. Wait for me over there. _____

Proofreading for Spelling

Read each sign. Find and circle the misspelled words.

1.
Plees do not feed
the bears.

5.
The zoo will close
todaiy at 4 PM.

2.
Spead Limit
55
Miles per Hour

6.
Leeve your
shoes outside.

3.
Stay on the traiyl.

7.
Stay out!
Wet paynt.

4.
Sweete tee $1.00
Peanuts $.50

8.
Do not be afrad
to try new things.

Write the misspelled words correctly on the lines below.

1. _____   5. _____

2. _____   6. _____

3. _____   7. _____

4. _____   8. _____

Spelling Words

Basic
1. lay
2. real
3. trail
4. sweet
5. today
6. dream
7. seem
8. tea
9. treat
10. afraid
11. leave
12. bait
13. screen
14. speed

Review
paint
please

Challenge
yesterday
explain

Connect to Writing

Too many short sentences make writing sound choppy.
Sometimes you can combine two short sentences to make
one longer compound sentence. Use a comma (,) and the
conjunction *and*, *but*, or *or* to form compound sentences.

Short Sentences	Compound Sentence
Libby owns many books. She hasn't read them all.	Libby owns many books, but she hasn't read them all.

Use a conjunction to form compound sentences.

1. Victoria came to our book party. She brought ten books.

_____

_____

2. We could hike on Saturday. We could wait until Sunday.

_____

_____

Correct these run-ons by using a conjunction to form compound sentences.

3. People could bring books they could bring magazines.

_____

_____

4. These books are very interesting they are hard to understand.

_____

_____

42

Long *o* Spelled *oa*, *ow*

Each word in the Word Bank is in the puzzle. Find and circle each word in the puzzle. Words can be across or down.

arrow	floating	undertow
below	goal	upload
blown	slow	
coach	throwing	

p	u	p	l	o	a	d	n	u	p
o	b	l	o	p	r	r	f	n	b
b	l	o	w	n	e	u	l	d	e
e	o	t	h	r	t	h	o	e	c
l	c	o	a	c	h	s	a	r	o
o	g	w	r	a	r	l	t	t	h
w	o	i	b	b	r	o	i	o	b
n	a	a	r	r	o	w	n	w	o
l	l	p	e	n	i	n	g	b	a
g	t	h	r	o	w	i	n	g	c

On a separate sheet of paper, use each word in the Word Bank in a sentence. Read your sentences aloud.

Identifying Nouns and Subjects

- A word that names a person, a place, or a thing is a **noun**. The noun that is doing something in a sentence is the subject.

    My <u>mom</u> helped to build the new <u>road</u>.

    The <u>work</u> lasted one <u>year</u>.

Thinking Questions
Is the word naming a person, a place, or a thing? Which noun tells who or what is doing something?

Write the two nouns in each sentence. Circle the subject of each sentence.

1. Workers brought in tables. _____

2. High winds knocked down the tents. _____

3. The sand blew into the food. _____

4. The moon was beautiful at night. _____

5. My family did some work. _____

6. My cousin showed the workers where to go.

_____

7. My brother played some music. _____

8. My uncle put up the signs. _____

9. Her mother brought food sometimes. _____

10. The mayor visited when the road was done.

_____

Long *o* Spelled *oa*, *ow*

Each word in the Word Bank is in the puzzle. Find and circle each word in the puzzle. Words can be across or down.

arrow	floating	undertow
below	goal	upload
blown	slow	
coach	throwing	

```
p u p l o a d n u p
o b l o p r r f n b
b l o w n e u l d e
e o t h r t h o e c
l c o a c h s a r o
o g w r a r l t t h
w o i b b r o i o b
n a a r r o w n w o
l l p e n i n g b a
g t h r o w i n g c
```

On a separate sheet of paper, use each word in the Word Bank in a sentence. Read your sentences aloud.

Identifying Nouns and Subjects

- A word that names a person, a place, or a thing is a **noun**. The noun that is doing something in a sentence is the subject.

  My <u>mom</u> helped to build the new <u>road</u>.

  The <u>work</u> lasted one <u>year</u>.

Thinking Questions
Is the word naming a person, a place, or a thing? Which noun tells who or what is doing something?

Write the two nouns in each sentence. Circle the subject of each sentence.

1. Workers brought in tables. _____

2. High winds knocked down the tents. _____

3. The sand blew into the food. _____

4. The moon was beautiful at night. _____

5. My family did some work. _____

6. My cousin showed the workers where to go.

_____

7. My brother played some music. _____

8. My uncle put up the signs. _____

9. Her mother brought food sometimes. _____

10. The mayor visited when the road was done.

_____

Name _____ Date _____

Capitalizing Nouns

- A word that names a person, place, or thing is a noun.

- **Common nouns** name any person, place, or thing. **Proper nouns** name a particular person, place, or thing.

- Proper nouns begin with capital letters and may have more than one word. People's titles and important words in titles of books are capitalized.

    His daughter <u>Audrey</u> visited <u>him</u> at his <u>job</u> in <u>England</u>.

Thinking Question
Does the noun name any person, place, or thing, or does it name a particular person, place, or thing?

Write *common* or *proper* for each underlined noun.

1. Outside of <u>Atlanta</u>, Jessie's father works in an office. _____

2. Bennie came to his father's bicycle <u>shop</u>. _____

3. Many parents invite their <u>children</u> to the places they work.

   _____

4. Mike went to <u>New York City</u> with his mother. _____

5. They saw a <u>parade</u> and ate great food. _____

6. Gary's father took him to an <u>Ice Age</u> display at the museum.

   _____

45

Spelling Word Sort

Pop's Bridge
Spelling:
Long *o* Spellings

Write each Basic Word under the correct heading.

Long *o* Spelled *o*	Long *o* Spelled *ow*
_____	_____
_____	_____
_____	_____
_____	_____
_____	_____

Long *o* Spelled *oa*

_____

_____

_____

_____

_____

Spelling Words

Basic
1. load
2. opening
3. told
4. yellow
5. soak
6. shadow
7. foam
8. follow
9. glow
10. sold
11. window
12. coach
13. almost
14. throat

Review
cold
most

Challenge
tomorrow
sailboats

Review: Add the Review Words to your Word Sort.

Challenge: Add the Challenge Words to your Word Sort.

Focus Trait: Development
Important and Interesting Details

Good writers use interesting details to develop their ideas.

For example:

The girl rode her bike.

The above sentence would be much more interesting with important details added:

The small redheaded girl proudly rode her shiny new yellow bike to school.

Read each sentence and look at the illustration from "Pop's Bridge" on the page listed. Add interesting details to each sentence.

1. Page 134: The family looked at the bridge.

_____

_____

2. Page 137: The boy shouted on the street.

_____

_____

3. Page 143: Robert was happy.

_____

_____

4. Page 144: He cut the puzzle piece.

_____

_____

Cumulative Review

Read each clue. Unscramble the letters and write the word that answers the clue. Read the words you made.

1. This is a food. Many people eat it in the morning.　　　mtoeala　　　_____

2. You might do this if you do not want to do something.　　　anlcopmi　　　_____

3. Cars drive fast on these kinds of roads. They have two or more lanes.　　　whgysiha　　　_____

4. This is a way to heat bread.　　　tasot　　　_____

5. This can take you across the sea, when it's windy.　　　alitabos　　　_____

6. This number is the answer to these math problems: 5 X 3 and 5 + 5 + 5.　　　efnietf　　　_____

7. There are four of these. They are winter, spring, summer, and fall.　　　eosnsas　　　_____

8. This is the color of a lemon.　　　lelwyo　　　_____

9. This describes something that never moves very quickly.　　　wols　　　_____

10. This can help you find your way when you are driving.　　　pdraaom　　　_____

Pop's Bridge

More Views from the Bridge

Mr. Shu, Charlie's dad, is writing a letter to his family in China about what it is like to work on the Golden Gate Bridge. Use the text and illustrations to help you write the letter.

Read page 130. What was it like to be a painter on the Golden Gate Bridge?

Dear Family,

I am working as a painter on the Golden Gate Bridge!

You would not believe how big it is! Guess what I do?

Every morning I

It is hard work to be a painter because

Sometimes I am afraid that

I really like being a painter on the bridge. It is

exciting work. I will tell you more when the bridge

is finally done.

Love to everyone,

Chang Shu

Charlie Shu has just been to the party at Robert's house to celebrate the opening day of the bridge. He is writing a journal entry about it.

Read pages 144–147. What was the party like for Charlie?

Today was opening day at the bridge! It was so thrilling. After we walked across the bridge, there was a big party at Robert's house.

There were a lot of people and food at the party. I felt _____

_____

Remember that puzzle we were doing? Robert had the missing piece all along! My dad and Robert's dad put the piece in together. This made me feel

_____

_____

For awhile I thought Robert believed his dad was better than mine. But now I know that

_____

_____

It was a really good day for a lot of reasons!

Name _____ Date _____

Common and Proper Nouns

Write the two nouns in each sentence. Circle the noun that is the subject of the sentence.

1. The boys watched the hotel being taken down. _____

2. A large ball knocked down the old walls. _____

3. A new building would go up in that space. _____

4. Soon, a huge hole was in the ground. _____

Write _common_ or _proper_ for each underlined noun.

5. We learned about the Rocky Mountains in school. _____

6. My aunt came all the way from Canada. _____

7. The crowd rode horses. _____

8. It was an exciting day. _____

Write the sentences correctly. Capitalize the appropriate underlined words.

9. We went with mrs. benitez to the museum of natural history.

   _____

10. We bought a book called animals in the wild.

   _____

Pop's Bridge
Spelling:
Long o Spellings

Long o Spellings

In the spaces below, write a Spelling Word to complete each newspaper ad.

1.

The Shoe Store is _____! Come in and try on a pair of our great shoes.

4.

Do you like baseball? Baseball _____ needed to work with children. Apply in person.

2.

_____ Washers We'll clean your glass!

5.

Garage Sale today and _____. _____ the signs to our house.

3.

Enjoy the _____ of a warm fire! Buy a _____ of our firewood.

6.

Store Closing Sale We cannot close until everything is _____.

Spelling Words

Basic
1. load
2. open
3. told
4. yellow
5. soak
6. shadow
7. foam
8. follow
9. glow
10. sold
11. window
12. coach
13. almost
14. throat

Review
cold
most

Challenge
tomorrow
sailboats

1. _____
2. _____
3. _____, _____
4. _____
5. _____, _____
6. _____

Name _____ Date _____

Lesson 4
READER'S NOTEBOOK

Pop's Bridge
Vocabulary Strategies:
Word Families

Word Families

Read each sentence. Use your understanding of the base word to figure out the meaning of the underlined word. Write the base word and the meaning of the underlined word.

1. The window display did not look good, so the crew had to <u>rethink</u> where to put the items.

   _____

2. The children were <u>clinging</u> to each other because of the cold wind.

   _____

3. The excitement over the team's win caused a <u>celebration</u> that lasted hours.

   _____

4. They <u>stretched</u> the rope across the yard.

   _____

5. As the day became <u>foggier</u>, it became impossible to see the mountains.

   _____

6. The player was balancing the basketball on one finger, spinning it <u>faster</u> and faster.

   _____

7. After another sock disappears, Dad buys a new package of <u>socks</u>.

   _____

8. It was <u>unbelievable</u> how close the water came during the high tide.

   _____

Name _____ Date _____

Lesson 4
READER'S NOTEBOOK

Pop's Bridge
Grammar:
Spiral Review

Compound Sentences

- A **compound sentence** is made up of two **simple sentences** joined by a comma followed by a **conjunction**.
- The words *and*, *but*, *or*, and *so* are conjunctions.
- Two simple sentences that run together without using a comma and a conjunction are called a **run-on** sentence.

> **Simple sentences:** Nina will go to the concert. She will go to the movies.
>
> **Run-on sentence:** Nina will go to the concert she will go to the movies.
>
> **Compound sentence:** Nina will go to the concert, or she will go to the movies.

Write the conjunction that best joins the two simple sentences into one compound sentence. Then write the compound sentence.

1. Roy wears his helmet. He wears his kneepads.

_____

2. Betsy will use her gloves. She will borrow a pair.

_____

Correct the run-on sentence by using a comma and a conjunction to form a compound sentence.

3. Riding is fun I like hiking better.

_____

4. We can ride today we can hike tomorrow.

_____

Proofreading for Spelling

Read the following newspaper article. Find and circle the misspelled words.

Spelling Words

Basic
1. load
2. open
3. told
4. yellow
5. soak
6. shadow
7. foam
8. follow
9. glow
10. sold
11. window
12. coach
13. almost
14. throat

Review
cold
most

Challenge
tomorrow
sailboats

Yelloaw Jackets Win First Game

The stadium was owpen for the game. Coch Smith and her players were ready. The game was sould out. Not even the coald weather kept people away. The crowd cheered as the team entered the stadium.

The first batter scored a run almowst right away. During the game, nine more players folloawed her lead. The Yellow Jackets left the other team in the shados.

A player towld me after the game that they intend to win every game this season. They will be put to the test tomorroaw when they play the Colts.

Write the misspelled words correctly on the lines below.

1. _____   6. _____

2. _____   7. _____

3. _____   8. _____

4. _____   9. _____

5. _____   10. _____

Connect to Writing

Using exact nouns helps make your writing clearer
and more interesting.

Less-Exact Noun	More-Exact Noun
road	superhighway
area	valley

**Replace each underlined noun in the sentences with a more exact
noun. Use the nouns in the word box.**

ranch	coyotes	ponies
thunderstorms	city	cowboys

1. Ernie saw two <u>men</u> through his binoculars. _____

2. They were rounding up some <u>animals</u>. _____

3. Off to one side, some <u>wild animals</u> were hard to see. _____

4. Faraway, the sky was filled with <u>rain</u>. _____

5. They worked hard to get people back to their <u>home</u>. _____

Correctly capitalize the proper noun, personal title, and book title.

6. (proper noun) new mexico _____

7. (personal title) mrs. lopez _____

8. (book title) amazing bridges from around the world

_____

Long *i* Spelled *i*, *ie*, *igh*

**Read each sentence. Choose the missing word from the box.
Write the word in the blank.**

find	climb	fried
sights	wild	lie
sigh	untied	
tried	midnight	

1. I did not _____ the book I was looking for.

2. The clock strikes twelve at _____.

3. Jasmine and her family went into the city to see the

_____.

4. The _____ animal ran through the forest.

5. I would like to _____ a mountain some day.

6. I tripped over my shoelaces because they were

_____.

7. The best dish at this restaurant is _____

chicken.

8. "I wish it would stop raining," Marty said with a

_____.

9. The police officer _____ to direct traffic.

10. George Washington once said, "I cannot tell a

_____."

Name _____ Date _____

Lesson 5
READER'S NOTEBOOK

Roberto Clemente

Grammar:
Plural Nouns with -s and -es

Identifying Singular and Plural Nouns

> • A noun that names only one person, place, or thing is a **singular noun**. A noun that names more than one person, place, or thing is a **plural noun**.
>
> • Add -s to most singular nouns to form the plural.
>
>   The children played a ball <u>game</u>.
>   The children played ball <u>games</u>.
>   They ran from place to <u>place</u>.
>   They ran to different <u>places</u>.

Thinking Question
Is the word naming only one person, place, or thing or is the word naming more than one person, place, or thing?

Write *singular* or *plural* for each underlined noun.

1. Many <u>kids</u> played ball games long ago. _____

2. The <u>ball</u> was made of cloth. _____

3. One player ran between two <u>stones</u>. _____

4. They would throw the ball at a <u>runner</u>. _____

Write the plural form of the noun in parentheses to complete the sentence.

5. Later, teams drew _____ on the field. (line)

6. Teams built _____ for another edge of the field. (wall)

7. Some _____ would throw the ball underhand. (pitcher)

8. Some games would last twelve _____. (hour)

Plural Nouns with *-s*

- Add *-s* to most nouns to form the plural.

Singular:	*team*	*cap*	*bat*
Plural:	*teams*	*caps*	*bats*

Thinking Question
Do I add -s to form the plural?

Write the plural form of the underlined noun.

1. They put a new <u>stain</u> on the floor.

   They tested two different _____ to see which would be darker.

2. Portia slipped and fell with a loud <u>bang</u>.

   A few minutes later, there were two louder _____.

3. The basketball <u>player</u> wore high-top sneakers.

   More _____ started wearing them after the first game.

4. The <u>light</u> came on when he fell into the switch.

   After three people fell, more _____ came on.

5. They put a <u>sign</u> on the ground to warn people not to slip.

   At the end of the day, there were a dozen _____ in that area.

Name _____ Date _____

Spelling Word Sort

Roberto Clemente

Spelling:
Long *i* Spellings

Write each Basic Word under the correct heading.

Long *i* Spelled *i*	Long *i* Spelled *ie*
_____	_____
_____	_____
_____	_____
_____	_____
_____	_____

Long *i* Spelled *igh*	
_____	_____
_____	_____
_____	_____

Review: Add the Review Words to your Word Sort.

Challenge: What letter or letters form the long *i* sound in the two Challenge Words?

_____ ; _____

Spelling Words

Basic
1. slight
2. mild
3. sight
4. pie
5. mind
6. tie
7. pilot
8. might
9. lie
10. tight
11. blind
12. fight
13. dies
14. midnight

Review
find
night

Challenge
silent
frightening

Focus Trait: Organization
Time-Order Words

Writers use transition words, or time-order words, to organize their writing and to show when events happen. For example:

<u>After they won</u> the championship game, all the boys on Pedro's soccer team cheered and high-fived each other. <u>Next</u>, they went out for pizza to celebrate.

Read the following paragraph. In each blank, fill in the phrase from the box that fits best.

Then	Yesterday morning
Afterwards	During the game
Before I left the house	When I got to the field

1. _____, I woke up with butterflies in my stomach. It was the day of my first softball game! Immediately, I jumped out of bed. **2.** _____ I put on my new uniform and ran downstairs for breakfast. **3.** _____, I reminded my mother to take the camera to the game. **4.** _____, my teammates were there practicing. **5.** _____, I got two hits and one run! In the end, we won the game by one point. **6.** _____, my mother took me out for ice cream.

Name _____ Date _____

Lesson 5
READER'S NOTEBOOK

Roberto Clemente

Phonics:
Cumulative Review

Cumulative Review

Write a word from the box to complete each sentence.

most	lightning	flowed
slimy	toast	railroad
tries	knights	
glowing	title	

1. Lava _____ down the sides of the volcano and into the sea.

2. A bolt of _____ suddenly flashed across the sky.

3. What is the _____ of your favorite book?

4. For breakfast, Karl likes to eat _____ with peanut butter.

5. I love to watch the fireflies _____ in the dark summer sky.

6. King Arthur and his _____ sat at a huge round table.

7. The worm felt _____ when I touched it.

8. Always stop, look, and listen before crossing a _____ track.

9. The athlete finally jumped over the bar after three _____.

10. Lee knew _____ of the answers on the test, but not all of them.

Reader's Guide

Roberto Clemente

1960 World Series Program

The Pittsburgh Pirates are going to play the
New York Yankees. Use examples from the text to
fill out each section of the program for famous hitter
Roberto Clemente.

**Read page 170. Use the information on this page to
tell how Clemente started out playing baseball.**

1960 World Series Pittsburgh Pirate Roberto Clemente
How Roberto Clemente Got Started
_____ _____ _____

**Read page 172. Use what you read to write about how
Clemente ended up in Pittsburgh. What was it like for him?**

Why Roberto Clemente Came to Pittsburgh
_____ _____ _____

Read pages 173–174. Why was Clemente's first game with the Pirates so important?

Roberto Clemente's First Game with the Pirates

_____

_____

_____

Read pages 175–176. Why did so many children love Roberto Clemente?

Roberto Clemente Has Many Fans

_____

_____

_____

Read page 177. How do you think Roberto Clemente felt right before the World Series? Why do you think he felt that way? Imagine you are Roberto Clemente and tell fans how you feel about playing in the World Series.

Roberto Clemente in His Own Words

_____

_____

_____

_____

Plural Nouns with *-s* and *-es*

Write *singular* or *plural* for each underlined noun.

1. The fans went to find their <u>seats</u>. _____

2. The popcorn seller brought them two <u>boxes</u>.

   _____

3. Other fans passed a giant <u>ball</u> around.

   _____

4. A foul ball sailed up into the stands from the <u>field</u>.

   _____

5. Some fans had special <u>passes</u> that let them go onto the

   field. _____

Write the plural form of the noun in parentheses to complete the sentence.

6. Two _____ had wire mesh that stopped foul
   balls. (fence)

7. People stood in the _____ instead of sitting
   in their seats. (aisle)

8. The fans clapped for a series of great _____
   of hard-hit balls. (catch)

9. The scoreboard could not show any _____,
   because that number was broken. (six)

10. There were _____ of programs to hand out
    to the fans. (stack)

Long *i* Spellings

Write a Basic Word to answer each question.

Roberto Clemente

Spelling:
Long *i* Spellings

1. If you were eating a round dessert with a flaky crust, what would you be eating? _____

2. What is the opposite of loose? _____

3. What is the time when one day ends and another begins? _____

4. What would a man wear around his neck if he was getting dressed up? _____

5. If you did not tell the truth, what did you tell?

   _____

6. Who flies a plane? _____

7. What do you think with? _____

8. What does a boxer have to do? _____

Spelling Words

Basic
1. slight
2. mild
3. sight
4. pie
5. mind
6. tie
7. pilot
8. might
9. lie
10. tight
11. blind
12. fight
13. die
14. midnight

Review
find
night

Challenge
silent
frightening

Roberto Clemente

Vocabulary Strategies:
Prefix *mis-*

Prefix *mis-*

Read the letter. Notice the underlined words. Write a reply to this letter. Use at least four of the underlined words in your letter.

Dear Friend,

    I did not mean to <u>misbehave</u> or to <u>mistreat</u> you. I thought it was funny when someone <u>mispronounced</u> your name. I didn't think it would upset you, but I can see that I <u>miscalculated</u> that. If someone said I did not want to be your friend, then they are <u>misinformed</u>. Can we please forget about this <u>misunderstanding</u>?

Your friend

_____

_____

_____

_____

_____

_____

_____

_____

_____

Commas in Sentences

- **Commas** are used in a date or when listing city and state in a sentence.
- Commas are also used when combining sentences and when using nouns or verbs in a series.

    On June 3, 1973, in Chicago, Illinois, they played baseball, football, and soccer.

Rewrite each sentence with a comma where it belongs in a date or a place.

1. They loaded the plane bringing supplies on December 29 1972.

_____

2. It was headed for Managua Nicaragua.

_____

Combine each group of sentences. Put the nouns or verbs in a series with commas. Write the new sentence.

3. The plane carried food. The plane carried water.
   The plane carried supplies.

_____

4. A pilot was onboard. A baseball star was onboard.
   A helper was onboard.

_____

Proofreading for Spelling

Find the misspelled words and circle them.

Plane Has Narrow Escape

A brave pielot saved the lives of her passengers yesterday when she saved an airplane from crashing.

Captain Jo Ann Foster was flying at 35,000 feet at midnite when her plane began to rock. There was only a sliet wind, so she knew her plane was in trouble. An engine was out, and the plane was sinking. Not only that, but thick fog made her have to fly blighnd. She was in a tite spot.

Captain Foster quickly thought of things she mite do. Different ideas went through her miend. She would have to fite to guide her plane to safety.

"I felt some miled fear," she said later, "but I was mainly thinking of how to save the plane and the passengers."

She found the nearest airport on the map and steered toward it. Finally, the airport came in siet. Captain Foster made a perfect landing, and 147 passengers were safe.

Spelling Words

Basic
1. slight
2. mild
3. sight
4. pie
5. mind
6. tie
7. pilot
8. might
9. lie
10. tight
11. blind
12. fight
13. die
14. midnight

Review
find
night

Challenge
silent
frightening

Write the misspelled words correctly on the lines below.

1. _____   6. _____

2. _____   7. _____

3. _____   8. _____

4. _____   9. _____

5. _____   10. _____

Name _____ Date _____

Lesson 5
READER'S NOTEBOOK

Roberto Clemente

Grammar:
Connect to Writing

Connect to Writing

Using the correct spelling of plural nouns makes your writing clearer and easier to understand. Add *-s* to form the plural of most singular nouns. Add *-es* to form the plural of a singular noun that ends with *s, sh, ch,* or *x.*

Sentences With Singular Nouns That Should be Plural Nouns	Sentences with Correct Plural Nouns
The baseball player tried two bat before choosing one.	The baseball player tried two bats before choosing one.
The teams sat on two bench.	The team sat on two benches.

Circle the singular noun that should be plural in each sentence. Then write the sentence using the plural spelling of the noun.

1. The fans rode to the baseball game in ten bus.

   _____

2. Most of the fans have already been to a few game this year.

   _____

3. Juan and Mary took their baseball glove to the game.

   _____

4. The pitcher made two great catch.

   _____

5. Another player made two good toss to first base.

   _____

VCV Words with Long and Short Vowels

**Read each sentence. Choose the missing word from the box.
Write the word. Then reread the complete sentence.**

visit	robot	flavor
tiny	limit	shiver
report	decide	gravel

1. We took a bumpy ride down a _____ road in the country.

2. Chocolate is my favorite _____ of ice cream.

3. I _____ the amount of sweets that I eat.

4. My sister has a collection of _____ glass animals.

5. I need to pick a topic for my _____.

6. It was hard to _____ which movie to watch.

7. The icy rain made me _____.

8. Steve hopes to _____ the Space Museum someday.

9. That interesting machine is called a _____.

Action Verbs

A word that tells what people or things do is a **verb**.
Words that show action, or something that is
done, are **action verbs**.

The owl **blinked** its eyes.

It **slept** in a hollow tree.

Thinking Question
*What is the subject
doing?*

Each sentence has one action verb. Write the action verb on
the line.

1. Some animals sleep during the day. _____

2. They look for food at night. _____

3. Owls see well in the dark. _____

4. The owl spread its wings wide. _____

5. Then it flew from the tree. _____

6. It beat its wings quietly. _____

7. The owl spotted a small mouse. _____

8. It swooped down for the mouse. _____

9. The mouse hid in a hollow log. _____

10. The owl returned to its tree. _____

Being Verbs

Some verbs do not show action. The verbs *am*, *is*, *are*, *was*, and *were* are examples of **being verbs.** They are forms of the verb *be*. They tell what someone or something is or was.

Thinking Question
What does the sentence tell me about what the subject is or was?

> I *am* interested in bats.
> I *was* proud of my knowledge of bats.
> They *are* amazing flyers.
> You *were* last at the zoo.
> He *is* skilled at identifying bats.
> We *were* excited at the zoo.

Am, *is*, and *are* show present tense. *Was* and *were* show past tense.

Write the being verb on the line. Write *present* or *past* for each verb.

1. My father was nice to my class. _____

2. He is kind and gives us his zoo passes. _____

3. We were thankful. _____

4. The boys are upset when they cannot go. _____

5. You are good to help us. _____

6. Most people are happy with the idea. _____

7. They were surprised when we asked. _____

8. They are annoyed sometimes but not often. _____

9. I am careful to ask nicely. _____

10. I was friendly to everyone. _____

Name _____ Date _____

Spelling Word Sort

Write each Basic Word in the box where it belongs. You will write words with two vowel sounds in more than one box.

Vowel sound in *rope*	Vowel sound in *meet*
_____	_____
_____	_____
_____	_____
_____	_____
Vowel sound in *came*	**Vowel sound in *bite***
_____	_____
_____	_____
_____	_____
Vowel sound in *blue*	**Vowel sound in *flat***
_____	_____
_____	_____
Vowel sound in *cup*	**Vowel sound in *dress***
_____	_____
Vowel sound in *skip*	**Vowel sound in *odd***
_____	_____
_____	_____

Spelling Words

Basic
1. math
2. toast
3. easy
4. socks
5. Friday
6. stuff
7. paid
8. cheese
9. June
10. elbow
11. program
12. shiny
13. piles
14. sticky

Review
each
both

Challenge
comb
holiday

Challenge: Add the Challenge Words to your Word Sort.

Focus Trait: Evidence
Details and Examples

Writer's Idea	Details and Examples
Bats hang upside down.	Bats' toes are shaped like hooks, so it's no effort for a bat to hang upside down.

A. Read each of the writer's ideas. Find the details and examples from *Bat Loves the Night* that help explain the idea. Complete the sentences.

Writer's Idea	Details and Examples
1. Bats use their wings like we use our arms and hands.	A bat's wing is its _____ and hand. Four _____ fingers _____ the skin of the wing.
2. Bats use sound to locate things in the dark.	She _____ her voice around her like a _____ , and the echoes come singing back. They carry a sound _____ of all her voice has touched.

B. Read the writer's idea. Look at the pages from *Bat Loves the Night*. Write details and examples that help explain the idea.

Pair/Share Work with a partner to find sentences in the story that include details and examples that support the writer's idea.

Writer's Idea	Details and Examples
3. Baby bats mature quickly.	

Cumulative Review

Write a word from the box to complete each sentence. Then read
the complete sentence.

pilot	planet	tiger
second	visit	bacon
flavor	finish	cabins

1. Can we play outside after we _____ our
   homework?

2. My cousins came to _____ us last summer.

3. As we were leaving the plane, the _____
   shook my hand.

4. The scouts stayed in small _____ near
   the lake.

5. Chocolate is the _____ of ice cream that
   I like best.

6. Would you like _____ with your eggs?

7. Look! That reddish light in the sky is the _____ Mars!

8. Brad came in _____ in the race, right
   behind Jay.

9. We watched a _____ sleep under the tree.

Bat Loves the Night

File a Missing Bat Report

One night you were looking out of your window with your binoculars when you saw a bat flying through the sky. Scientists who are tracking the bat want some information, and you have that information. Fill out this missing bat report using information from the text.

> **Read pages 212–214. What was the first thing you saw the bat do when you looked out the window?**
>
> _____
>
> _____
>
> **Read pages 215–217. Someone reported the bat was swooping and gliding through the sky. What do you think she was doing?**
>
> _____
>
> _____
>
> **Read pages 218–219. We have evidence that a moth showed up at some point. Did you see what happened? Tell us, step by step.**
>
> First, _____
>
> Then, _____
>
> Finally, _____

Read pages 220–221. You are the only one to see where the bat went next. Describe what happened.

_____

_____

Read pages 222–224. We suspect that there are baby bats living in the barn. Tell us everything you know about the babies.

_____

_____

Read page 225. Now we think we know where the bat is. What do you think the bat is doing? When can we see this bat again?

_____

_____

Name _____ Date _____

Action Verbs and Being Verbs

There is one action verb in each sentence. Write the verb on the line.

1. Randy looked for a book about bats. _____

2. He found one in the back shelf. _____

3. He searched for new facts. _____

4. He learned that bats do not live in Antarctica. _____

5. He borrowed the book. _____

Write the being verb on the line. Then write *present* or *past*.

6. We are interested in nature. _____

7. You were thoughtful to bring the binoculars. _____

8. I am able to see through the binoculars. _____

9. We are tired of walking in the heat. _____

10. The bats were hidden in the caves. _____

Name _____ Date _____

More Short and Long Vowels

Write the Basic Words that match each heading.

Proper Nouns

1. _____

2. _____

Common Nouns

3. _____   7. _____

4. _____   8. _____

5. _____   9. _____

6. _____   10. _____

Describing Words

11. _____

12. _____

13. _____

Verb

14. _____

On the line below, write a sentence using one word from each group above.

15. _____

_____

Spelling Words

Basic
1. math
2. toast
3. easy
4. socks
5. Friday
6. stuff
7. paid
8. cheese
9. June
10. elbow
11. program
12. shiny
13. piles
14. sticky

Review
each
both

Challenge
comb
holiday

Name _____ Date _____

Lesson 6
READER'S NOTEBOOK

Bat Loves the Night
Vocabulary Strategies:
Suffixes -able, -ible

Suffixes -*able*, -*ible*

**Write a sentence using the words provided. Make sure the
sentence helps the reader understand the meaning of the word.**

1. agreeable

_____

2. valuable

_____

3. reversible

_____

4. comfortable

_____

5. breakable

_____

6. sensible

_____

7. spreadable

_____

8. flexible

_____

Complete Subjects and Predicates

- A sentence is a group of words that tells a complete thought and has a complete subject and a complete predicate.
- The **subject** tells whom or what the sentence is about and usually comes at the beginning of the sentence.
- The **predicate** tells what the subject does or is, and it can be one word or more than one word.

    Many different words   tell about the same idea.
    Subject   **Predicate**

Write the subject or the predicate of each sentence.

1. Tommy cut pictures from the magazine. (subject) _____

2. He and his friends glued them to a poster. (predicate)

_____

Combine each pair of sentences. Use a conjunction to form a compound subject in each new sentence. Write the new sentence on the line.

3. My friends gathered magazines about animals. The teachers gathered magazines about animals.

_____

4. The kids carried the magazines. The teachers carried the magazines.

_____

82

Proofreading for Spelling

Bat Loves the Night
Spelling:
More Short and Long Vowels

Find the misspelled words and circle them.

Jun 1: This was a great day! It started out like
any other Frieday. I did all the usual stufe. I
got dressed, put on my shoes and soks, and ate
some tost and jam. But as I started to coamb my
hair, I herd kids playing outside. For a minute, I
thought it might be a holliday. Then suddenly
I remembered that school is out. This is the first
day of summer vacation! There are no more
mathe tests, no more pils of homework, and no
more long days of sitting still.

The rest of the day was perfect. I played
kickball with my friends, rode my bike, and went
to the pool. It was so much fun that I think I'll do
it all again tomorrow. Or maybe I'll just read
a book and take it eazy. I <u>love</u> summer!

Spelling Words

Basic
1. math
2. toast
3. easy
4. socks
5. Friday
6. stuff
7. paid
8. cheese
9. June
10. elbow
11. program
12. shiny
13. piles
14. sticky

Review
each
both

Challenge
comb
holiday

Write the misspelled words correctly on the lines below.

1. _____   6. _____

2. _____   7. _____

3. _____   8. _____

4. _____   9. _____

5. _____   10. _____

Name _____ Date _____

Lesson 6
READER'S NOTEBOOK

Bat Loves the Night
Grammar:
Connect to Writing

Connect to Writing

If the subject you are writing about is doing more than one
action, you can tell about it in one sentence. You can combine
more than one simple predicate to form a compound predicate.
This can help make your sentences longer and less choppy.

Short Sentences with Simple Predicates	Longer, Smoother Sentence with Compound Predicate
Bat opens her eyes. Bat twitches her ears.	Bat opens her eyes and twitches her ears.
My father saw a bat. My father took a picture of it.	My father saw a bat and took a picture of it.

**Combine each pair of sentences. Use a compound predicate in
each new sentence. Write the new sentence on the line.**

1. I like to read about bats. I like to write stories about them.

   _____

2. The bat flew by the streetlight. The bat soared toward the pond.

   _____

3. My brother drew a picture of a bat. My brother gave it to me.

   _____

4. I found a book about bats in the library. I brought it home.

   _____

Three-Letter Clusters

**Read each question and choose an answer from the box.
Write the word.**

screwdriver	springtime	strongest
throne	scrubbing	unscramble
sprinkler	thrilling	streetlight

1. What do you call the person who can lift the heaviest load? _____

2. What lights the neighborhood on nights when there is no moon in the sky? _____

3. How would it feel to have an audience stand and applaud for you? _____

4. When do most trees grow new leaves? _____

5. What helps grass grow when there is no rain? _____

6. What is kept in a toolbox and can help put things together? _____

7. What is the best way to get dirty hands clean?

   _____

8. What is a queen's chair called? _____

9. How can you make a word from a set of mixed-up letters? _____

Name _____ Date _____

Lesson 7
READER'S NOTEBOOK

What Do Illustrators Do?
Grammar:
Verb Tenses

Present and Past Tense

Many verbs in the **present tense** have an -s ending with a singular subject. Many verbs in the present tense do not have an -s ending with a plural subject. Most verbs in the **past tense** have an -ed ending.

Thinking Question
In what tense does the action of the verb occur, and what ending does the verb have?

An artist <u>paints</u> paintings.	present
Artists <u>paint</u> paintings.	present
An artist <u>painted</u> paintings yesterday.	past

**Write *present* if the underlined verb shows the present tense.
Write *past* if the underlined verb shows the past tense.**

1. Our class <u>gathers</u> pages for a book. _____

2. We <u>combined</u> them into a small book. _____

3. We <u>fold</u> some pages in two. _____

4. Other students <u>traced</u> lines for borders. _____

5. Carmen <u>cuts</u> the rough edges. _____

6. Walt and John <u>iron</u> the pages flat. _____

7. Some older kids <u>poked</u> holes in the page.

_____

8. One group <u>ties</u> string through the holes. _____

9. The string <u>pulled</u> the pages together. _____

10. In the last step, we <u>cover</u> it with thick paper.

_____

Name _____ Date _____

Lesson 7
READER'S NOTEBOOK

What Do Illustrators Do?
Grammar:
Verb Tenses

Present, Past, and Future Tense

Many verbs in the **present tense** with singular subjects use an -s ending. Verbs in the present tense with plural subjects do not use an ending.

Many verbs in the **past tense** use an -ed ending.

Verbs in the **future tense** use the helping verb *will*.

Thinking Question
In what tense does the action of the verb occur, and what ending does the verb have?

The artist <u>paints</u> a curving line.	present
The artists <u>paint</u> a curving line.	present
The artist <u>painted</u> a curving line.	past
The artist <u>will paint</u> a curving line.	future

Write *present* if the underlined verb shows present tense. Write *past* if the underlined verb shows past tense. Write *future* if the underlined verb shows future tense.

1. My friends and I <u>walked</u> to the library. _____

2. We <u>will search</u> for interesting picture books. _____

3. Lora <u>flips</u> through many books. _____

4. Kitty <u>stacked</u> the books that we liked. _____

5. Roberto and Vera <u>look</u> for the best ones. _____

6. Quentin <u>will place</u> a marker at the colorful ones.

   _____

7. Tory <u>loves</u> art with bright colors. _____

8. Walt <u>prefers</u> art drawn with colored pencils. _____

Spelling Word Sort

Write each Basic Word in the box where it belongs.

scr	*spr*
_____	_____
_____	_____
_____	_____
_____	_____

str	*thr*
_____	_____
_____	_____
_____	_____
_____	_____

Challenge: Add the Challenge Words to your Word Sort.

Spelling Words

Basic
1. three
2. scrap
3. street
4. spring
5. thrill
6. scream
7. strange
8. throw
9. string
10. scrape
11. spray
12. threw
13. strong
14. scratch

Review
think
they

Challenge
straight
scramble

Name _____ Date _____

Lesson 7
READER'S NOTEBOOK

What Do Illustrators Do?
Writing:
Opinion Writing

Focus Trait: Purpose
Topic Sentence

Good writers of opinion paragraphs include a topic sentence that states an opinion. The topic sentence helps readers understand the writer's purpose for writing. This makes an opinion stronger and more convincing. Compare the following sentences.

Weak Topic Sentence: Illustrators work on drawings.

Strong Topic Sentence: Illustrators often do very interesting work.

Read each paragraph. Revise the topic sentence in each paragraph to state an opinion.

1. Have you thought about composting leaves in the fall? That means you put the leaves in a pile instead of in the trash. The leaves eventually break down and can be added to gardening beds.

   _____

   _____

2. Many people exercise. Exercise helps people maintain a healthy weight. It also gives people more energy throughout the day.

   _____

   _____

Name _____ Date _____

Cumulative Review

Lesson 7
READER'S NOTEBOOK

What Do Illustrators Do?
Phonics: Cumulative Review

Write words from the box to complete each paragraph.

threw	scratched	strong
screen	through	described
stretched	screamed	strange

Ray couldn't find the key to his house. He _____ 1 _____ his head and tried to remember where he had seen it last. He went to the school office and _____ 2 _____ his lost key chain. The clerk looked _____ 3 _____ the Lost and Found box and found the key chain. Ray was grateful that someone had turned in his key!

***

Emily shivered as she looked out the window into the dark, foggy night. Suddenly she heard a _____ 4 _____ noise coming from the back yard! She tiptoed to the back of the house and pushed open the _____ 5 _____ door. She heard someone pound on the house and say, "Boo!" Emily _____ 6 _____. Then her brother stepped into the light and they both laughed.

***

There was once a troll so mean and so tough that no one in the village was _____ 7 _____ enough to fight him. The villagers _____ 8 _____ out a huge net on the ground and hid next to their houses. When the troll came to town and stepped onto the net, the people wrapped him up, carried him out of town, and _____ 9 _____ him into a big mud puddle. The troll never came back!

Name _____ Date _____

Lesson 7
READER'S NOTEBOOK

What Do
Illustrators Do?
Independent Reading

 Reader's Guide

What Do Illustrators Do?

A Comic Book Guide to Illustrated Books

Now that you know what illustrators do, you can write about it in your own comic. Use examples from the text to help explain how an illustrated book is made.

Create a comic using the cat and the dog that watched as the illustrations were created.

Draw and write what illustrators do. Use details from page 246 for Step 1 and page 247 for Step 2.

Step 1   Step 2

Name _____ Date _____

Lesson 7
READER'S NOTEBOOK

What Do
Illustrators Do?
Independent Reading

Read page 251. What do illustrators do to help them draw faces? Use what you learned to have the dog tell the cat two details from page 251 about drawing faces.

How Illustrators Draw Faces

Read page 258. In this comic, draw the cat talking about what she learned from the cover of *Jacqueline & the Magic Bean*. What does this cover tell you about the story?

Jacqueline & the Magic Bean

Name _____ Date _____

Lesson 7
READER'S NOTEBOOK

What Do Illustrators Do?
Grammar:
Verb Tenses

Present, Past, and Future Tense

Write *present* if the underlined verb shows present tense.
Write *past* if the underlined verb shows past tense.

1. Bill, the artist, <u>selects</u> a wall for art. _____

2. He <u>looked</u> everywhere for a good wall. _____

3. Some kids <u>live</u> near this wall. _____

4. The owner <u>allowed</u> us to paint it. _____

5. Bill <u>climbs</u> on a tall ladder. _____

Write *present* if the underlined verb shows present tense. Write *past* if the underlined verb shows past tense. Write *future* if the underlined verb shows future tense.

6. The artist <u>will measure</u> the wall first. _____

7. The colors <u>drip</u> down the wall. _____

8. Someone else <u>painted</u> this wall long ago. _____

9. When it is done, people <u>will enjoy</u> the wall. _____

10. The new art <u>stretches</u> high into the sky. _____

Three-Letter Clusters

Write the Basic Word that is an antonym of the underlined word in each sentence.

1. Why did you choose such a <u>common</u> costume?

2. My uncle helped me learn how to <u>catch</u> a ball.

3. The <u>fall</u> is my favorite time of year.

4. Please <u>spread</u> the mud from your boots before coming in.

5. The surprise party was a big <u>bore</u> for me!

6. Are you <u>weak</u> enough to lift this heavy box?

7. Don't <u>whisper</u> in the library.

8. Everyone <u>caught</u> confetti to celebrate the new year.

1. _____	5. _____
2. _____	6. _____
3. _____	7. _____
4. _____	8. _____

Challenge: Write a word that means the opposite of each Challenge Word.

9. _____

10. _____

Use one of the Challenge Words and its antonym in a sentence.

11. _____

Spelling Words

Basic
1. three
2. scrap
3. street
4. spring
5. thrill
6. scream
7. strange
8. throw
9. string
10. scrape
11. spray
12. threw
13. strong
14. scratch

Review
think
they

Challenge
straight
scramble

Synonyms

sketch	large	see	enormous
view	show	illustrate	exhibit
polite	pleasant		

Read each word below. Write the two synonyms from above that have almost the same meaning as the word.

1. display

_____

2. huge

_____

3. nice

_____

4. observe

_____

5. draw

_____

Choose one set of synonyms. Write a sentence or two for each word to show the difference in the shades of meaning.

6. _____

_____

_____

_____

_____

Name _____ Date _____

Lesson 7
READER'S NOTEBOOK

What Do Illustrators Do?
Grammar:
Spiral Review

Kinds of Sentences

- There are four kinds of sentences.

  The art is wonderful.   **Declarative** (statement)

  Who made that piece?   **Interrogative** (question)

  Pick up the mess you made.   **Imperative** (command)

  What a bold color she used!   **Exclamatory** (exclamation)

Write *statement* if the sentence tells something. Write *question* if the sentence asks something.

1. We walked outside to paint. _____

2. Who is going to come with us? _____

3. Why are we going outside? _____

**Write *command* if the sentence tells someone to do something.
Write *exclamation* if the sentence shows strong feeling.**

4. Painting outside is fun! _____

5. Do not spill paint out here. _____

6. Create a painting with bold colors. _____

Proofreading for Spelling

Find the misspelled words and circle them.

Spelling Words

War of the Giants

Coming Soon!

In the sterange world of the future, giant animals roam the earth. But what happens when the beasts come together in the last city on Earth? See these thee monsters clash in the biggest battle of all time!

Birdzilla   This giant bird has claws srong enough to skratch through solid rock. It is headed steraight for the city!

The Ape King   When angry, this towering ape can lift a car off the steet and thow it into the air. People skream and run. But can they get away?

The Night Croc   This huge crocodile waits at the edge of town. When you least expect it, he will sping out of the dark and attack. This movie is filled with thills and surprises.

Don't Miss It!

Basic
1. three
2. scrap
3. street
4. spring
5. thrill
6. scream
7. strange
8. throw
9. string
10. scrape
11. spray
12. threw
13. strong
14. scratch

Review
think
they

Challenge
straight
scramble

Write the misspelled words correctly on the lines below.

1. _____   6. _____

2. _____   7. _____

3. _____   8. _____

4. _____   9. _____

5. _____   10. _____

Connect to Writing

If all of the action in a paragraph happens during the
same time, keep the verbs in the same tense.

Incorrect Paragraph

   Next year, I will take an art class. Other students and I paint
pictures of one another. We will study drawing and painting.

Correct Paragraph

   Next year, I will take an art class. Other students and I will paint
pictures of one another. We will study drawing and painting.

**Read this paragraph. Change each underlined verb to make it
match the tense of the other verbs. Write the new sentences on
the lines below.**

   Maybe twenty years from now, cars will be very different
than they are now. Drivers <u>enter</u> an address into a computer.
The car will go to that place, and the driver will be able
to read or take a nap! Cars <u>serve</u> drinks and snacks. Cars
<u>slow down</u> automatically when there is a stop sign ahead.
All cars <u>run</u> on energy from the sun. Cars of the future <u>have</u>
exciting features!

1. _____

2. _____

3. _____

4. _____

5. _____

Name _____ Date _____

Lesson 8
READER'S NOTEBOOK

Silent Letters *kn, wr*

The Harvest Birds
Phonics:
Silent Letters *kn, wr*

Read each line of the poem. Choose the missing word
from the box. Write the word.

wring	wrists	knight
wrapped	knot	wrong
kneel	wrinkles	knee

Handy Things to Remember

To keep a gift a secret, keep it _____ and out of sight.
₁

To fight a pesky dragon, call a strong and fearless _____!
₂

If one string isn't long enough, get two and make a _____.
₃

To get the answers right, not _____, remember what you're
₄

taught.

To make a wet sponge dry, you need to _____ it out.
₅

Hold it tightly with both hands and twist your _____ about.
₆

Wear _____ pads when you're skating to keep from getting hurt.
₇

To look your best, make sure there are no _____ in your shirt.
₈

If you _____ in an anthill, stand up as quickly as you can.
₉

If you forget these handy tips, just read them all again!

Name _____ Date _____

Lesson 8
READER'S NOTEBOOK

The Harvest Birds
Grammar:
Using Commas

Commas in a Series of Nouns

A series is a list of three or more words used in a sentence. Use **commas** to separate three or more nouns included in a series. Commas tell readers when to pause.

Juan grew beans, corn, and tomatoes.

Thinking Question
Are there three or more words listed together in the sentence?

Write each sentence correctly. Add commas where they are needed.

1. Jamal Tina and Ed want to write their own folktales.

_____

2. Their class is having a contest for plays poems and folktales.

_____

3. The friends read stories on Monday Tuesday and Wednesday.

_____

4. Jamal read folktales about crows fish and cats.

_____

5. Tina likes the folktales of England Spain and Mexico.

_____

6. Folktales can take place in deserts jungles and cities.

_____

Commas in a Series of Verbs

A **series** is a list of three or more words used in a sentence. Use commas to separate three or more verbs included in a series. Commas tell readers when to pause.

Juan planted, watered, and harvested vegetables.

Thinking Question
Are there three or more words listed in the sentence?

Write each sentence correctly. Add commas where they are needed. If no commas are needed, write *No Commas* on the line.

1. I plan write and correct my folktale.

_____

2. The animals in my story walk talk and snore.

_____

3. My friends listened laughed and clapped as I read my story.

_____

4. A snake trapped and tried to eat a frog in Ron's folktale.

_____

5. The frog danced jumped and ran away from the snake.

_____

Spelling Word Sort

Write each Basic Word in the web where it belongs.

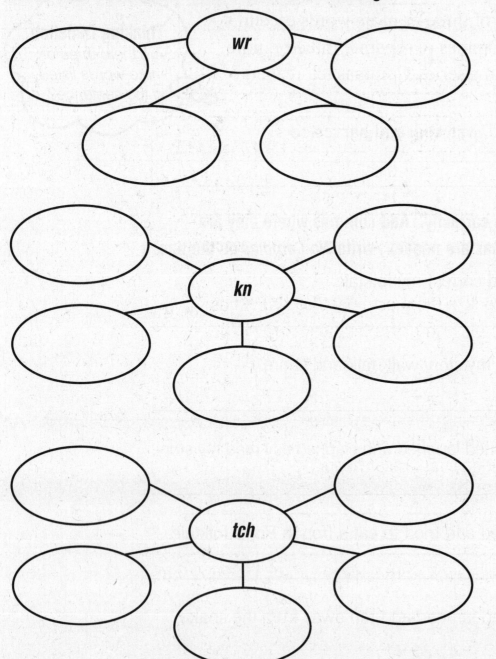

Spelling Words

Basic
1. itch
2. wreck
3. knee
4. patch
5. wrap
6. knot
7. watch
8. knife
9. stretch
10. write
11. knew
12. knock
13. match
14. wrong

Review
know
catch

Challenge
wrinkle
knuckle

Challenge: Add the Challenge Words to your Word Sort. Write each one near the correct group, and draw a line to connect it to the web.

Name _____ Date _____

Lesson 8
READER'S NOTEBOOK

The Harvest Birds
Writing:
Opinion Writing

Focus Trait: Elaboration
Using Linking Words

Linking words and phrases can connect supporting
reasons to opinions in a paragraph. This makes the
author's ideas easier to understand.

Linking Words	
because therefore	since for example

**Rewrite each passage so a linking word or phrase connects the
reason to the opinion.**

1. The male peacock is the most beautiful bird. It has
shimmering purple and green feathers.

_____

_____

2. Our zoo has animals from many places. It has rare
orangutans, pandas, and polar bears.

_____

_____

3. The garden in our back yard is unusual. We built it on
a hill.

_____

_____

4. Our pumpkin was the best in the fair. It won first place.

_____

_____

Name _____ Date _____

Lesson 8
READER'S NOTEBOOK

The Harvest Birds

Phonics:
Cumulative Review

Cumulative Review

Write words from the box to complete the lines of the play.

know	wrong	wrote
threw	knees	through
knickknacks	wrap	knocked

Granny and the Rascal

Granny Gopher: Who _____ over my beautiful vase?

Rascal Raccoon: Why are you so upset about a silly old vase? You have

plenty of other _____ sitting around.

Granny Gopher: That vase was special. Great-Granny Gopher gave it to
me. Now, is there something you'd like to confess?

Rascal Raccoon: I _____ that you think I broke that vase,
but I never went near it.

Granny Gopher: That's what you said after you _____ a

baseball _____ my window.

Rascal Raccoon: You were _____ about that, too.

Granny Gopher: There were witnesses to that crime. Skunk and Rabbit

_____ me a note saying they *saw* you break the window.

Rascal Raccoon: You can't trust what those tattle-tales say!

Granny Gopher: You can at least clean up this broken glass. It's hard for

me to get down on my sore old _____ to do a job like this.

Rascal Raccoon: Uh, sure, Granny Gopher. I have to _____

a present for Rabbit's birthday party right now. But I'll stop by and help you

later. *I promise!*

The Harvest Birds

A Radio Interview

The harvest birds have come in for a special radio interview. They saw everything that happened to Juan Zanate, and they are ready to tell his story. Use details from the text to answer the interviewer's questions.

Read pages 285–292.

Interviewer: Juan Zanate was looking for land for a long time. Finally, Grandpa Chon agreed to give him some. You were there and saw what happened next. Please explain what happened.

Harvest Birds: _____

_____

_____

_____

_____

Interviewer: Why did the farmers laugh at Juan Zanate?

Harvest Birds: _____

_____

_____

_____

Read pages 293–297.

Interviewer: Juan had a great harvest at the end of the summer. How did people react to this?

Harvest Birds: _____

_____

Interviewer: Now just between us, what is your secret?

Harvest Birds: _____

_____

Interviewer: Well, thank you, harvest birds! I think we have a better understanding of Juan Zanate now. Is there anything you would like to add?

Harvest Birds: _____

_____

Commas in Addresses

> • Use a comma to separate each part of an address.
>   Susan Henley, 29 Wylie Lane, Ocoee, Florida

Write each address correctly. Add commas where they are needed.

1. Tammy Ruiz 14 Silver Brook Road Dallas Texas

_____

2. Wayne Thomas 1170 South Pleasant Street Belding Michigan

_____

3. The package is going to Dave Layler 73 Bent Road Remsen New York.

_____

4. My friend lives at 87 Moore Avenue Glendale California.

_____

5. We are moving to 60 Myrtle Street Addis Louisiana.

_____

6. The letter is from Lucy Rawly 170 Adobe Way Albuquerque New Mexico.

_____

Name _____ Date _____

Lesson 8
READER'S NOTEBOOK

The Harvest Birds
Spelling:
Unexpected Consonant Spellings

Unexpected Consonant Spellings

Write the Basic Word that best completes each sentence.

1. Your elbow and your _____ are both body parts that can bend.

2. A pair of scissors and a _____ are both tools for cutting.

3. To share a story, you can tell it to someone or

   _____ it down.

4. Two things that can have a flame are a candle and a

   _____.

5. To tell the time, you can look at a clock or check your

   _____.

6. To let someone know you're at the door, ring the

   bell or _____.

7. You can tie a bow or just tie a _____.

8. A rubber band and bubble gum are both things

   that can _____.

Challenge: Name something that is similar to a knuckle. Then
write to tell how the two things are alike.

9. _____

10. _____

_____

Spelling Words

Basic
1. itch
2. wreck
3. knee
4. patch
5. wrap
6. knot
7. watch
8. knife
9. stretch
10. write
11. knew
12. knock
13. match
14. wrong

Review
know
catch

Challenge
wrinkle
knuckle

108

Name _____ Date _____

Lesson 8
READER'S NOTEBOOK

The Harvest Birds
Vocabulary Strategies:
Context Clues

Context Clues

Read each sentence. Use context clues to figure out the meaning of the underlined word. Use a dictionary to check that your meanings are correct.

1. Did you <u>note</u> our meeting on your calendar?

_____

2. We needed another <u>yard</u> of yarn to finish the sewing project.

_____

3. I didn't win, but I didn't feel <u>bitter</u> about it.

_____

4. She always hangs up her coat, so it was odd that she <u>misplaced</u> it.

_____

5. The <u>shallow</u> bowl only held a little bit of water.

_____

6. Tina was <u>mortified</u> when she fell in front of the school.

_____

Name _____ Date _____

Lesson 8
READER'S NOTEBOOK

The Harvest Birds
Grammar:
Spiral Review

Sentence Fragments

A **sentence** is a group of words that tells a complete thought. It tells who or what, and it tells an action or state of being.

A man planted seeds in his garden.

Write the group of words that will complete each sentence.

1. A bird _____.

   lives in the tree   on the fence

2. Rabbits _____

   soft and cute   like to eat garden vegetables

3. _____ are vegetable eaters.

   Rabbits   Usually

4. _____ ate the whole garden of flowers.

   Broke through a fence   A herd of goats

For each item, combine the two fragments to write a complete sentence.

5. A bird is. a clever but shy animal.

   _____

6. A garden needs. a fence that can keep animals out.

   _____

Proofreading for Spelling

Find the misspelled words and circle them.

Lost Hiker Rescued on Big Pine Trail

Thanks to her own quick thinking, 10-year-old Rosa Gomez was rescued along Big Pine Trail on Saturday. The girl had stopped to wach a group of deer and lost her hiking group. She tried to catch up but took the rong trail. Rosa new she was lost and wanted to leave clues to help someone find her. She decided to rite her name in the dirt with a stick each time she took a turn. The girl had to stop after she fell on a rocky area. Her nuckles were scraped and her nee was badly cut. To stop the bleeding, Rosa used her pocket nife to cut a strip from her sweatshirt. She used the cloth to rap the injury and tie a not just as she had learned to do in first-aid training. The minutes began to strech into hours, but Rosa stayed calm. Rescuers found her just before dark.

Spelling Words

1. itch
2. wreck
3. knee
4. patch
5. wrap
6. knot
7. watch
8. knife
9. stretch
10. write
11. knew
12. knock
13. match
14. wrong

Review
know
catch

Challenge
wrinkle
knuckle

Write the misspelled words correctly on the lines below.

1. _____   6. _____

2. _____   7. _____

3. _____   8. _____

4. _____   9. _____

5. _____   10. _____

Connect to Writing

You can combine short, choppy sentences to make your writing smoother. You can combine sentences by **joining single words in a series.** You use commas to separate the nouns or verbs in a series. Remember to add *and* after the last comma.

Short, Choppy Sentences	Longer, Smoother Sentence
Carla watched crows. Carla watched gulls. Carla watched pigeons.	Carla watched crows, gulls, and pigeons.

Combine three short, choppy sentences by joining nouns or verbs in a series. Write the new sentence on the line.

1.

The crows in the story walked.	The crows in the story laughed.	The crows in the story talked.

_____

2.

Carla told Ramon about the crows.	Carla told Ed about the crows.	Carla told Lisa about the crows.

_____

3.

The crows perched on branches.	The crows perched on wires.	The crows perched on rooftops.

_____

4.

Ramon played with the birds.	Ramon laughed with the birds.	Ramon sang with the birds.

_____

Vowel Diphthongs *ow* and *ou*

Read each sentence. Choose the missing word from the box.
Write the word.

crowded	rowdy	outdoors
found	showers	sunflower
howling	doghouse	shouted

1. As soon as the rain stopped, the children hurried

   _____ to play.

2. When a wolf is _____, you can hear it from
   far away.

3. Our poodle Fifi sleeps in her _____, where it
   is warm and dry.

4. When the birthday girl came in, everyone jumped up and

   _____, "Surprise!"

5. Will it be sunny today, or will we have _____?

6. The _____ seeds that we planted grew into
   tall plants with bright yellow blooms.

7. Carl still hasn't _____ the jacket that he lost
   last month.

8. The bus was so _____ that a lot of riders
   had to stand up.

9. If the children get too _____, they might
   wake the baby.

Abstract Nouns

> **Thinking Questions**
> *Does the noun name an idea, a feeling, or a quality?*

- A **noun** can name a person, place, or thing. This kind of noun is a **concrete noun**.

- A noun can also name an idea, a feeling, or a quality. This is called an **abstract noun**. You cannot see, hear, taste, smell, or touch an abstract noun.

  He listened in the <u>hope</u> of hearing a new story.

  It was just <u>luck</u> that he arrived in time.

A noun in each sentence is underlined. Write *abstract* if the noun names an idea, a feeling, or a quality. Write *concrete* if it is a noun you can see, hear, taste, smell, or touch.

1. The younger men enjoyed the older man's <u>friendship</u>.

_____

2. The old man found <u>strength</u> in being among friends.

_____

3. The friends took <u>delight</u> in listening to the old man's

stories. _____

4. One story was about a silly <u>king</u>. _____

5. The crowd's <u>laughter</u> pleased the old man. _____

6. It gave him <u>energy</u> to tell another story.

_____

Abstract Nouns

A noun that names an idea, a feeling, or a quality is
an **abstract noun**. You cannot see, hear, taste, smell, or
touch an abstract noun.

The couple did not have much <u>wealth</u>.

Their <u>joy</u> was obvious for everyone to see.

Thinking Question
*Does the noun name
an idea, a feeling, or
a quality?*

**The word in parentheses tells whether the abstract noun in the
sentence names an idea, a feeling, or a quality. Write the noun.**

1. He took delight in keeping the audience in suspense.

(feeling) _____

2. He told the story with complete honesty.

(quality) _____

Write a sentence for each abstract noun.

3. beauty

_____

_____

4. childhood

_____

_____

Spelling Word Sort

Write each Basic Word in the correct list.

<u>mou</u>th	<u>dow</u>n
_____	_____
_____	_____
_____	_____
_____	_____
_____	_____
_____	_____
_____	_____

Challenge: Add the Challenge Words to your Word Sort.

Spelling Words

Basic
1. clown
2. round
3. bow
4. cloud
5. power
6. crown
7. thousand
8. crowd
9. sound
10. count
11. powder
12. blouse
13. frown
14. pound

Review
house
found

Challenge
mountain
coward

Focus Trait: Organization
Order of Reasons

When you provide an opinion, be sure to begin your answer by stating your opinion clearly. Use words from the question in your opinion statement. Then provide reasons in order. List the strongest reason first.

EXAMPLE:

Question: In *Kamishibai Man*, why do you think the old man and his wife call each other "Grandma" and "Grandpa" although they have no children of their own?

Strong Opening and Reasons: I think the old man and his wife call each other "Grandma" and "Grandpa" because they wish they had children and grandchildren. They are also older in age.

Read each question about *Kamishibai Man*. Write a strong opening sentence that clearly states your opinion. Then provide reasons in order. List the strongest reason first.

1. | **Question:** Why do you think the children were always happy to see the kamishibai man?
   |
   | **Opinion Statement and Reasons:**

2. | **Question:** Why do you think the little boy ran away from the kamishibai man?
   |
   | **Opinion Statement and Reasons:**

Cumulative Review

Write a word from the box to complete each rhyme.

clown	cow	kneel	pout	wreck
count	crown	knight	powder	write

1. You're going to have to _____ to change that wheel.

2. A princess wears a gown with her _____.

3. Please add some chili _____ to the chowder.

4. Why would you paint a frown on a _____?

5. You won't see that _____ lose a fight.

6. When you're dressed as a scout, do not _____.

7. The lady hurt her neck in the _____.

8. Be careful with that plow around the _____.

9. You should get this amount when you _____.

10. Before you start to _____, turn on a light.

Kamishibai Man

A New Point of View:
The Boy Who Didn't Like Candy

When I was a boy, I listened to the stories of the kamishibai man every day. Help me tell his story with details from the text and illustrations.

Read pages 324–326. Why was the old man surprised?

_____

_____

_____

_____

Read pages 328–330. Why was the old man happy?

_____

_____

_____

Read page 332. Why did I run away from the kamishibai man when I was a little boy?

_____

_____

_____

Read page 333–334. How did television change things?

_____

_____

_____

Read page 338. What happened when the large crowd gathered?

_____

_____

_____

Name _____ Date _____

Lesson 9
READER'S NOTEBOOK

Kamishibai Man
Grammar:
Abstract Nouns

Abstract Nouns

> • The subject of a sentence is a noun. It can be concrete or abstract.
>
> • A noun that names an idea, a feeling, or a quality is an **abstract noun**.
>
>   In the story, the girls formed a friendship.

Two nouns in each sentence are underlined. Circle the subject of the sentence. Write the abstract noun.

1. The story begins with memories of a missing locket.

   _____

2. A letter had information about the locket.

   _____

3. The girls had confidence in themselves.

   _____

4. After several hours, Annette had success and found the

   locket. _____

Choose two abstract nouns from above and write a sentence with them.

5. _____

   _____

Lesson 9
READER'S NOTEBOOK

Vowel Sound in *town*

Kamishibai Man
Spelling:
Vowel Sound in *town*

Write the Basic Word that best replaces the underlined word or words in each sentence.

1. The man wears a <u>ring of gold and jewels on his head</u> to show he is king.

2. The actress waved to the <u>large group of people</u> as she walked by.

3. The angry bees made a loud buzzing <u>noise</u>.

4. Her brother's teasing made Marta <u>put an unhappy look on her face</u>.

5. Let's <u>say the numbers in order</u> as Justin jumps the rope.

6. A <u>performer in a silly costume</u> gave out balloons to all the children.

7. That gray <u>puffy shape in the sky</u> looks like it might bring rain.

8. For my birthday, I had a <u>circle-shaped</u> cake decorated to look like a soccer ball.

1. _____	5. _____
2. _____	6. _____
3. _____	7. _____
4. _____	8. _____

Spelling Words

Basic
1. clown
2. round
3. bow
4. cloud
5. power
6. crown
7. thousand
8. crowd
9. sound
10. count
11. powder
12. blouse
13. frown
14. pound

Review
house
found

Challenge
mountain
coward

Challenge: On another sheet of paper, write a one-paragraph story using both Challenge Words and one or more Basic Words.

Name _____ Date _____

Lesson 9
READER'S NOTEBOOK

Kamishibai Man
Vocabulary Strategies:
Dictionary/Glossary

Dictionary/Glossary

Read each word. Find each word in a print or digital
dictionary. Complete the chart.

Word	Part(s) of Speech	Word with Endings
1. jewel		
2. rickety		
3. blast		
4. sharp		
5. blur		

Now write one sentence of your own that could be an example
sentence for one meaning of each word.

1. _____

2. _____

3. _____

4. _____

5. _____

Name _____ Date _____

Lesson 9
READER'S NOTEBOOK

Kamishibai Man
Grammar:
Spiral Review

Writing Titles and Addresses

- Begin the first, last, and each important word in a book or story title with a capital letter. Example: Reptiles on the Road
- Capitalize a person's title when it is in front of his or her name. Example: Detective Ruiz
- Use a comma to separate each part of an address. Example: Ken Lopez, 530 Sandy Lane, Hialeah, Florida

Capitalize each title correctly.

1. I checked out swimming with the dolphins from the library.

   _____

2. He listened to coach Taylor speak.

   _____

3. Her story is called "never listen to a gerbil."

   _____

4. The book a great leader is about president Washington.

   _____

Write each address correctly. Add commas where they are needed.

5. Sam Johnson 22 Meadowlark Avenue Houston Texas

   _____

6. She moved to 749 South Lake Road Spokane Washington.

   _____

Name _____ Date _____

Proofreading for Spelling

Find the misspelled words and circle them.

Dear Uncle Tony,

Thanks for the circus tickets that you sent.
I can always cownt on you to make my birthday
a lot of fun! I really enjoyed the elephant act. The
biggest one must have weighed a thausand pownds.

The acrobat show was great, too. No one made
a sownd while one acrobat carried his partner over
the tightrope. When they came down, they leaped
through a rownd hoop that was on fire. The crawd
went crazy! Then, a cloun pretended he was going
to do the same thing, but he was too scared. His
buddies laughed at him as if he was a big couward.
Finally, he jumped through the hoop and his pants
caught fire. When he took his bouw, he saw the
clowd of smoke behind him. It was really funny.

I hope that next time you come to town, we can
all go to the circus together!

Love,
Gina

Spelling Words

Basic
 1. clown
 2. round
 3. bow
 4. cloud
 5. power
 6. crown
 7. thousand
 8. crowd
 9. sound
 10. count
 11. powder
 12. blouse
 13. frown
 14. pound

Review
house
found

Challenge
mountain
coward

Write the misspelled words correctly on the lines below.

1. _____   6. _____

2. _____   7. _____

3. _____   8. _____

4. _____   9. _____

5. _____   10. _____

Name _____ Date _____

Lesson 9
READER'S NOTEBOOK

Kamishibai Man
Grammar:
Connect to Writing

Connect to Writing

Exact nouns are used to make your writing clearer and more interesting.

Noun	Exact Noun
The story filled Linda with happiness.	The story filled Linda with delight.
His actions showed his kindness.	His actions showed his compassion.

Replace each underlined noun in the sentences with a more exact noun. Use the nouns in the word box.

joy	doubt
panic	bravery

1. Jen felt <u>uncertainty</u> about telling her story to strangers.

_____

2. Her <u>fear</u> grew as more people arrived. _____

3. Seeing her best friend in the audience gave her <u>courage</u>.

_____

4. In the story, the characters felt <u>happiness</u> about the

coming circus. _____

Name _____ Date _____

Lesson 10
READER'S NOTEBOOK

Young Thomas Edison
Phonics: Words with
au, *aw*, *al*, and *o*

Words with *au*, *aw*, *al*, and *o*

Read each sentence and choose an answer from the box. Write the word. Then read the sentence aloud.

tablecloth	yawning	offered
sauce	faucet	bossy
false	awesome	mall

1. To save water, be sure to fix a leaky _____

as soon as possible.

2. We went shopping at the _____ and

had lunch at the Food Court.

3. My _____ cousin Cindy makes her

brothers do everything her way.

4. Pete had homemade yogurt with raspberry _____

on top.

5. On our test, we had to tell whether each statement was

true or _____.

6. The desert sunset was an _____ sight!

7. Coach Simms _____ to help me work on my pitch.

8. The gravy spilled and stained our best _____.

9. Are the girls _____ because they are

tired or because they are bored?

Subject Pronouns

A **pronoun** is a word that can take the place of one or more nouns in a sentence. The pronouns *I, you, he, she, it, we,* and *they* are **subject pronouns**. Pronouns can be singular or plural. A noun and the subject pronoun that replaces it must match each other in singular and plural forms.

Thinking Question
What pronoun can replace and match a noun or nouns in a sentence?

The telegraph was important.	It was important.
Samuel Morse invented it.	He invented it.
Our class learned this.	We learned this.

Write each sentence. Replace the underlined word or words with a subject pronoun.

1. Samuel Morse was born in Massachusetts.

   _____

2. Lucretia Walker became his wife.

   _____

3. The couple had two children.

   _____

4. Painting was another thing Morse did well.

   _____

5. The students and I enjoyed learning about him.

   _____

Object Pronouns

The **pronouns** *me*, *you*, *him*, *her*, *it*, *us*, and *them* are called **object pronouns**. Object pronouns follow action verbs and words like *to*, *for*, *at*, *of*, and *with*. A noun and the object pronoun, or **antecedent**, that replaces it must match each other in singular and plural forms.

- The pronouns *it* and *you* are both **subject pronouns** and object pronouns.

Nikola Tesla helped invent <u>radio</u>.
Nikola Tesla helped invent <u>it</u>.

Others worked with <u>Tesla</u>.
Others worked with <u>him</u>.

> **Thinking Question**
> *What pronoun replaces and matches one or more nouns that are the objects in a sentence?*

Write each sentence. Replace the underlined word or words with an object pronoun.

1. A man named Marconi worked on <u>wireless communication</u>.

_____

2. He helped make <u>radios</u> popular.

_____

3. Marconi married <u>Beatrice O'Brien</u> in 1905.

_____

4. Other people said they had invented <u>the system</u>.

_____

5. People are grateful to <u>Marconi</u> for what he did.

_____

Name _____   Date _____

Spelling Word Sort

Young Thomas Edison
Spelling
Vowel Sound in *talk*

Write each Basic Word where it belongs in the chart.

s<u>o</u>ft	p<u>aw</u>
_____	_____
_____	_____
_____	_____
_____	_____
_____	_____

f<u>al</u>l
_____
_____
_____
_____
_____

Challenge: Add the Challenge Words to your Word Sort.

Spelling Words

Basic
 1. talk
 2. cross
 3. awful
 4. law
 5. cloth
 6. cost
 7. crawl
 8. chalk
 9. also
10. raw
11. salt
12. wall
13. lawn
14. always

Review
soft
small

Challenge
often
strawberry

Focus Trait: Conventions
Avoiding Redundancy

Good writers introduce a new idea in each sentence. This writer crossed out a sentence that repeats an idea and wrote a new idea.

Thomas Edison loved to read. He would spend the entire day at the library. He wanted to read every book in the library. He would start at the last book on the shelf and work back to the first. ~~Edison wanted to read all of the books there.~~

New idea: *He would dream about his next experiment as he read.*

Read each paragraph. Cross out the sentence that repeats an idea. Write a new idea.

1. Thomas Edison was a very creative child. He created a laboratory in the cellar of his home. He would mix chemicals there. He would do this in the cellar. He also asked questions so that he could learn about things.

New Idea: _____

2. Edison's mother was important in his life. She educated him at home. She taught him very well there. She also encouraged him to learn for himself.

New Idea: _____

3. Edison invented many helpful things. He invented the carbon transmitter, which made voices sound louder. He invented the light bulb. This invention helped people. He even invented the motion picture.

New Idea: _____

_____

Cumulative Review

Write words from the box to complete the sentences.

cause	walkie-talkies	squawked
officer	foggy	already
paws	fault	flossing

1. My friend and I used _____ to communicate.

2. Brushing and _____ keep teeth healthy.

3. The chicken _____ loudly and flapped

   its wings.

4. The police _____ directed traffic when the

   lights were not working.

5. Dr. Ross finally figured out the _____ of

   the baby's fever.

6. When Tasha arrived, the game had _____

   started.

7. It was so _____ that I could barely see

   my neighbor's house.

8. It was my _____ that the library book

   got torn.

9. The kitten is all black except for its four white

   _____.

Reader's Guide

Young Thomas Edison

A Tour of the Thomas Edison Museum

Welcome to the Thomas Edison Museum! I am a tour guide for the museum. Help me take our visitors on a tour. We will explore Thomas Edison's early life by looking at some objects.

Read page 362.

This is a bottle from Thomas Edison's childhood. Why is it here in the museum?

_____

_____

_____

Read page 366.

Here you can see an old newspaper from when Thomas Edison was twelve years old. Why is it here in the museum?

_____

_____

_____

Read page 372.

Here is a photograph of an old locomotive. Why is it in the Thomas Edison museum?

_____

_____

_____

Read page 376.

Here is the last letter Thomas Edison received from his mother in 1869. Why is it here?

_____

_____

_____

Read pages 379–381.

Now if you step into the final room of the museum, you will see all of Thomas Edison's famous inventions! Why was he known as "The Wizard"?

_____

_____

_____

Thank you for taking a tour of the Thomas Edison Museum. It has been my pleasure to be your guide!

Name _____ Date _____

Lesson 10
READER'S NOTEBOOK

Young Thomas Edison
Grammar:
Pronouns and Antecedents

Pronoun-Antecedent Agreement

- A pronoun can take the place of one or more nouns in a sentence.

- An **antecedent** is the noun or noun phrase to which a pronoun refers. An antecedent usually comes before the pronoun, but it may come after. Pronouns and antecedents must agree in number, person, and gender.

  <u>Raul</u> thought about <u>his</u> invention.

  <u>Maggie</u> thought about <u>her</u> invention.

  <u>Raul and Maggie</u> thought about <u>their</u> inventions.

Complete each sentence by writing the pronoun that agrees with the underlined antecedent. Remember to make sure the pronoun and antecedent match in number, person, and gender.

1. Kevin checked out an <u>invention book</u> because

   _____ had a lot of information.

2. <u>I</u> said, "Show _____ the book."

3. <u>Maggie</u> typed up the notes _____ wrote about the invention.

4. <u>The students</u> felt _____ had done a great job.

5. <u>Ms. Jones</u> said _____ was proud of the students' hard work.

6. After _____ was done, <u>Raul</u> went home.

Name _____ Date _____

Lesson 10
READER'S NOTEBOOK

Young Thomas Edison
Spelling:
Vowel Sound in *talk*

Vowel Sound in *talk*

Read the titles and lists below. Write the Basic Word that belongs in each blank.

1. Things to Look for Before You _____: cars,

trucks, bicycles

2. Ways to Communicate: draw a picture, use sign

language, _____

3. Writing Tools: pencil, pen, _____

4. Things That Are Against the _____:
littering, speeding, stealing

5. Spices and Seasonings: garlic, cinnamon,

_____

6. Things People Eat _____: apples,
lettuce, tomatoes

7. Parts of a Building: staircase, window,

_____

8. Things Made of _____: shirt, scarf, sheet

Challenge: Write two lists similar to those above. Include a
Challenge Word in each title or list.

Spelling Words

Basic
1. talk
2. cross
3. awful
4. law
5. cloth
6. cost
7. crawl
8. chalk
9. also
10. raw
11. salt
12. wall
13. lawn
14. always

Review
soft
small

Challenge
often
strawberry

Name _____ Date _____

Lesson 10
READER'S NOTEBOOK

Young Thomas Edison
Vocabulary Strategies:
Shades of Meaning

Shades of Meaning

For each set of related words, write them in order on the arrows
to show the shades of meanings of the words. If necessary, look
up unfamiliar words in a dictionary before completing the arrows.

1. believe, suspect, think

⟵——————————————————————————⟶

2. happy, elated, content

⟵——————————————————————————⟶

3. angry, upset, furious, annoyed

⟵——————————————————————————⟶

4. scorching, hot, warm

⟵——————————————————————————⟶

5. glance, look, glare, stare

⟵——————————————————————————⟶

6. excited, exhilarated, enthusiastic

⟵——————————————————————————⟶

Name _____ Date _____

Lesson 10
READER'S NOTEBOOK

Young Thomas Edison
Grammar:
Spiral Review

Singular and Plural Nouns

- A noun that names only one person, place, or thing is a **singular noun**.
- A noun that names more than one person, place, or thing is a **plural noun**.
- Add -*s* to most singular nouns to form the plural.
- Add -*es* to form the plural of a singular noun that ends in -*s*, -*sh*, -*ch*, or -*x*.

    Students have invented <u>things</u> for many of their school <u>classes</u>.

Write singular or plural for each underlined noun.

1. An <u>invention</u> is like a lightbulb lighting up in your head.

    _____

2. Before, my <u>thoughts</u> were in the dark. _____

3. I don't know how a new <u>idea</u> comes to me. _____

4. I phoned two <u>friends</u> about my idea. _____

5. I will give them two <u>guesses</u> about what it is.

    _____

Use proofreading marks to change the underlined nouns from singular nouns to plural nouns.

Thank you for the <u>idea</u> <u>box</u> that you sent. We should meet to talk about the <u>invention</u> we are thinking about. I shared your <u>thought</u> with my <u>brother</u>.

Name _____ Date _____

Proofreading for Spelling

Find the misspelled words and circle them.

This morning was auful. I wanted to sleep late, but my brother kept whining. He was crawss because Mom wouldn't let him go out and play unless I went with him. I olways have to babysit! All I wanted was a little sleep. Since when is that against the lauw? Anyway, I took Ben out to play. I stretched out on the laun to relax, but before long Ben just had to crol over and bug me. He doesn't tawk very well yet, but I know what "jump game" means. Ben auften watches me play hopscotch and thinks it looks funny. I got some chawk and drew a board on the sidewalk. Ben laughed when I hopped on the squares. Then he was bored again. He wanted to swing. He aulso wanted a drink of water. When Ben finally took his nap, I ran to Ana's house. I'm going to sleep over tonight. Maybe I'll get to sleep late at *her* house!

Spelling Words

Basic
1. talk
2. cross
3. awful
4. law
5. cloth
6. cost
7. crawl
8. chalk
9. also
10. raw
11. salt
12. wall
13. lawn
14. always

Review
soft
small

Challenge
often
strawberry

Write the misspelled words correctly on the lines below.

1. _____   6. _____

2. _____   7. _____

3. _____   8. _____

4. _____   9. _____

5. _____   10. _____

Name _____ Date _____

Lesson 10
READER'S NOTEBOOK

Young Thomas Edison
Grammar:
Connect to Writing

Connect to Writing

Using a pronoun in place of a noun helps to avoid repeating words.

Repeated Nouns	Better Sentences
In 1806, Thomas Young thought of the phonograph. Later, Leon Scott improved the phonograph. Thomas Edison made the phonograph work.	In 1806, Thomas Young thought of the phonograph. Later, Leon Scott improved it. Thomas Edison made it work.

Rewrite each item. Use pronouns in place of repeated nouns.

1. The first phonograph did not play records. The first phonograph put sounds on a tin tube. Sounds entered the first phonograph through a bell.

   _____

   _____

2. Later, phonographs played records. These records were flat rings of wax. A needle cut sound into the records.

   _____

   _____

3. Bell and Tainter made their phonograph in 1886. Bell and Tainter called their phonograph a gramophone. The government gave its approval to Bell and Tainter.

   _____

   _____

   _____

Name _____ Date _____

Unit 2
READER'S NOTEBOOK

Amos and Boris
Segment 1
Independent Reading

Reader's Guide

Amos and Boris

Postcard to Pearl

Help Amos send a postcard to his friend, Pearl, telling her about his travel plans. Use the text and illustrations to describe the most important details about Amos and his boat. Then, use this information to write the postcard.

Read pages 3–5. Why did Amos love where he lived?

_____

_____

Why did Amos decide to build a boat?

_____

_____

What did Amos do when the boat was finished, before setting sail?

_____

_____

How do you think Amos felt before setting sail?

_____

_____

Name _____ Date _____

Now, use your answers to write the postcard. On the front, draw a picture of Amos and his boat. On the back, write a note from Amos to Pearl. Describe his plans for the boat and where he wants to go.

Front of Postcard

Dear Pearl,

_____

_____

_____

_____

_____

_____

_____
                            Love, Amos

TO:

Pearl M. Friend

333 Cheddar Street

Cheesetown, USA

32¢

Back of Postcard

Name _____ Date _____

Unit 2
READER'S NOTEBOOK

Amos and Boris
Segment 1
Independent Reading

From Amos's Journal

Amos kept a journal during his time on the boat. Use the text and illustrations to help fill out his journal entries.

Read page 6. What was the weather like when Amos started out? How did he feel at first?

September 6

_____

_____

Read page 7. How did Amos feel on his first day out at sea?

September 7

_____

_____

How did Amos feel after the first day?

September 8

_____

_____

Name _____ Date _____

Read page 9. What are some things Amos saw while lying on the deck of his boat?

September 9

_____

_____

How did Amos feel when he was lying on the deck of his boat?

Later that night …

_____

_____

What do you think Amos's last thoughts were before he unexpectedly fell into the sea? Write his final journal entry.

Even later that night …

_____

_____

Message in a Bottle

Imagine that Amos found his pen and paper with him in the water. Quickly, he wrote a message for help and put it in a bottle. First, use the text and illustrations to explain what happened. Then use that information to write Amos's message in a bottle.

Read page 9. How did Amos fall off his boat?

_____

_____

Read page 10. What did Amos do when he first fell off the boat?

_____

_____

Read page 11. What happened to Amos next?

_____

_____

What was Amos worried about?

_____

_____

Name _____ Date _____

Use your answers to write Amos's message in a bottle.
Describe what happened to him and why he needs help.

Reader's Guide

Amos and Boris

Best Friend Award

After his adventures with Boris, Amos
decided to give Boris a Best Friend Award.

Read page 12.
How did Amos feel before Boris found him?

_____

_____

Read pages 13–15.
How did Amos feel when he first met Boris?

_____

_____

Read pages 18–19.
What was it like for Amos traveling on Boris's back?

_____

_____

Read page 20.
How did Amos feel when it was time to say goodbye to Boris?

_____

_____

Name _____ Date _____

Unit 2
READER'S NOTEBOOK

Amos and Boris
Segment 2
Independent Reading

Design a Best Friend Award for Boris from Amos.
On the award, write why Boris is a good friend.
Use details from the story.

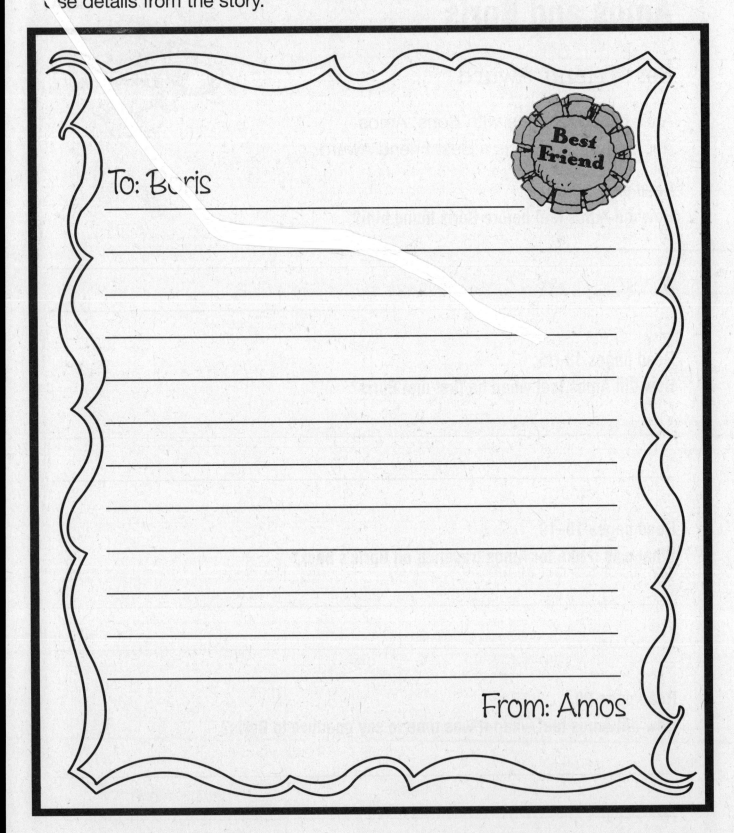

To: Boris

Best
Friend

From: Amos

Name _____ Date _____

Boris's Speech

Boris is going to give a speech at the Meeting of the Whales about his adventures with Amos. Use the text and illustrations to answer questions about the events. Then, use your answers to write the speech.

Read page 13. How did Boris first meet Amos?

_____

_____

What did Boris first think about Amos when he saw him?

_____

_____

Read page 14. Where did Boris first want to take Amos?

_____

_____

How did Amos feel about this?

_____

_____

Read page 15.
What did Boris decide to do with Amos next?

_____

_____

Read pages 16–17.
What made Amos angry?

_____

_____

How did Amos and Boris solve this problem?

_____

_____

Name _____ Date _____

Unit 2
READER'S NOTEBOOK

Amos and Boris
Segment 2
Independent Reading

Read pages 18–19.

What happened over the next week?

_____

_____

_____

Read page 20.

What happened on the last day that Boris and Amos were together?

_____

_____

_____

Read page 21.

What happened after Boris left Amos at his home?

_____

_____

_____

Now use your answers to write Boris's speech.
The speech should describe the events from
Boris's point of view.

Speech for the Meeting of Whales

_____

_____

_____

_____

_____

_____

_____

_____

_____

Name _____ Date _____

Unit 2
READER'S NOTEBOOK

Amos and Boris
Segment 3
Independent Reading

Reader's Guide

Amos and Boris

Interview with the Elephants

Imagine you are one of the elephants from
the story and you are being interviewed
for a radio program about Boris's rescue.

Read pages 22–23.
Tell me, Elephant, how did it all start?

_____

_____

Read page 24.
What happened when Amos, the mouse, came down to the beach?

_____

_____

**What do you think it was like when Amos
and Boris first saw each other again?**

_____

_____

Name _____   Date _____

Unit 2
READER'S NOTEBOOK

Amos and Boris
Segment 3
Independent Reading

Read page 25. How do you think Boris felt when he saw Amos run off like that?

_____

_____

Read pages 26–28. That is where you come into the story. What did Amos say when he ran up to you?

_____

_____

How did you feel when you first saw Boris lying there on the beach?

_____

_____

What did you and your friend decide to do to help Boris?

_____

_____

_____

Name _____ Date _____

Unit 2
READER'S NOTEBOOK

Amos and Boris
Segment 3
Independent Reading

Read pages 29–30.
What happened when you finally pushed Boris in the water?

_____

_____

What was it like when Boris and Amos had to say goodbye?

_____

_____

How did you feel while they said goodbye?

_____

_____

Thank you, Elephant, for that interview about
the great rescue of Boris the Whale!

Name _____ Date _____

Unit 2
READER'S NOTEBOOK

Amos and Boris
Segment 3
Independent Reading

One More Adventure

First, Boris saved Amos. Then, Amos helped save Boris. What if Boris and Amos had one more adventure? Write about what might happen next to the two friends. First, answer these questions about how the story ended.

Read page 30.
How do you think Boris felt at the end of the book?

_____

_____

How do you think Amos felt at the end of the book?

_____

_____

Do you think they would ever meet again? Why or why not?

_____

_____

Name _____ Date _____

Unit 2
READER'S NOTEBOOK

Amos and Boris
Segment 3
Independent Reading

Now think of another adventure for Amos and Boris.
Plan your story below.

Who are the characters in your story?

_____

_____

_____

What is the setting?

_____

_____

_____

What problem do the characters have? How do they solve it?

_____

_____

_____

Name _____ Date _____

Unit 2
READER'S NOTEBOOK

Amos and Boris
Segment 3
Independent Reading

Write your Amos and Boris story.
Draw a picture to go with it.

Vowel Diphthongs *oi, oy*

Read each sentence. Choose the missing word from the box.
Write the word. Then reread the complete sentence.

broiling	ointment	soy
coiled	oyster	disappoint
voyage	avoid	hoist

1. While hiking, Debra saw a snake _____ up on the path.

2. Before you can go sailing, you have to

   _____ the sails.

3. Steve made sure to get his mom a birthday card so that

   he would not _____ her.

4. My bike has a flat tire because I could not

   _____ the broken glass on the sidewalk.

5. Christine cooked the hotdogs by _____ them.

6. My grandmother is making a _____ around the world.

7. I don't like seafood, so I did not eat the _____.

8. Gwen put some _____ on her poison ivy rash.

9. My mom eats burgers that are made with

   _____ instead of meat.

Lesson 11
READER'S NOTEBOOK

**Technology Wins
the Game**

Grammar:
More Plural Nouns

Changing *y* to *i*

- Add -*s* or -*es* to most singular nouns to form **regular plural nouns.**
- If a noun ends with a consonant and *y*, change the *y* to *i*, and add -*es* to form the plural.

  Singular: *family*   *party*

  Plural: *families*   *parties*

Thinking Question
Does the noun end with a consonant and y?

Write the plural form of each singular noun in parentheses. Then write a new sentence using the plural form of the noun.

1. My teammates and I play basketball in many _____. (city)

   _____

2. We once played against a team that had _____ on their shirts. (pony)

   _____

3. Another team had two _____ on their shirts. (butterfly)

   _____

4. The teams are not really _____. (enemy)

   _____

5. I made _____ of the photos I took of the games. (copy)

   _____

Name _____ Date _____

Lesson 11
READER'S NOTEBOOK

Technology Wins the Game
Grammar:
More Plural Nouns

Irregular Plural Nouns

- The spelling of **irregular plural nouns** changes in a special way.

    The <u>woman</u> wanted to be as tall as the other <u>women</u>.

- The spelling of some nouns does not change when they are plural.

    That black <u>sheep</u> is as large as all the other <u>sheep</u>.

- The noun *woman* changes to *women* when it is plural.

- The noun *sheep* remains *sheep* when it is plural.

Thinking Questions
Does the noun add -s or -es to form a plural, or does it change its spelling? Does its spelling not change?

Write the plural form of the noun in parentheses to complete each sentence.

1. Tara grew up to be stronger than most other _____. (woman)

2. She was taller than most of the other _____ her age. (child)

3. As she grew, she could run faster than most _____. (deer)

4. Every fall she ran through the _____. (leaf)

5. She ran and won many races against _____. (man)

6. She lived on a farm with ducks and _____. (goose)

Name _____ Date _____

Vowel Sound in *joy*

Write each Basic Word under the correct heading.

Vowel Sound in *joy* spelled *oi*	Vowel Sound in *joy* spelled *oy*
_____	_____
_____	_____
_____	_____
_____	_____
_____	_____
_____	_____
_____	_____
_____	_____
_____	_____
_____	_____

Challenge: Add the Challenge Words to your Word Sort.

Spelling Words

Basic

1. joy
2. point
3. voice
4. join
5. oil
6. coin
7. noise
8. spoil
9. toy
10. joint
11. boy
12. soil
13. choice
14. boil

Review
come
are

Challenge
poison
destroy

Focus Trait: Elaboration
Signal Words

Cause	Effect
Amy practiced every day	won race

Sentence: <u>Because</u> Amy practiced every day, she won the race.

Read each cause and effect. Use a signal word to fill in the blank.

Cause	Effect
1. bought new running shoes	Cal's feet don't hurt
2. skier gets lost	sensor sends information

Sentence:

1. Cal bought new running shoes _____ his feet don't hurt.

2. _____ a skier gets lost, a sensor sends information.

Cause	Effect
3. tennis racket lighter	player can hit ball harder
4. Jana runs on grass	sometimes slips when it rains
5. water is cold	Max wears bodysuit

Sentence:

3. _____

4. _____

5. _____

Name _____ Date _____

Lesson 11
READER'S NOTEBOOK

Technology Wins the Game
Phonics:
Cumulative Review

Cumulative Review

Write a word from the box to complete each sentence. Then read the complete sentence.

royal	cowboy	pointy
enjoy	avoid	voyage
oiled	loyal	noisy

1. The men working outside my window were so

_____ that I could not fall asleep.

2. Theresa is a _____ friend, so I know I can
trust her.

3. Marc knew that his trip around the world would be the

_____ of a lifetime.

4. The metal lid was rusted shut because no one had

_____ it for years.

5. A king and a queen are _____ rulers.

6. Victor is mad at me, so he is trying to _____
talking to me.

7. If you _____ funny movies, you will love
this one!

8. Once I get some fake _____ ears, my elf
costume will be complete.

9. Randy loved taking horseback riding lessons because it

made him feel like a _____.

Technology Wins the Game

Sports Equipment Instruction Manual

You are writing a step-by-step manual that tells how sports equipment is made using the latest technology. It also explains how technology has changed over the years. Use information from the text to write the manual.

Read page 407. How are tennis balls made?

HOW TO MAKE A TENNIS BALL

Step 1: _____

Step 2: _____

Step 3: _____

Step 4: _____

Read page 408. How have vaulting poles changed over time?

THE HISTORY OF VAULTING POLES

First, _____

Next, _____

Then, _____

Today, _____

It took years to come up with the best technology for vaulting poles. But fiberglass is the best material because

_____

Read page 410. How have running shoes changed over time? Use the text and the timeline to fill in the manual page.

THE HISTORY OF RUNNING SHOES

First, _____

Next, _____

Next, _____

Next, _____

Today, _____

_____

Read page 412. How have football helmets changed over time?

THE HISTORY OF FOOTBALL HELMETS

First, _____

Next, _____

Then, _____

Next, _____

Next, _____

Today, _____

_____

The newest technology for football helmets is computer chips. These help because _____

_____

_____

_____

Name _____ Date _____

Lesson 11
READER'S NOTEBOOK

Technology Wins the Game
Grammar:
More Plural Nouns

Irregular Plural Nouns

Write the plural form of each singular noun in parentheses.

1. two tiny _____ (baby)

2. four long _____ (story)

3. twelve ripe _____(cherry)

4. fresh red _____ (berry)

5. eight cute _____ (puppy)

Write *singular* or *plural* for each underlined noun.

6. Many <u>women</u> play sports. _____

7. Many <u>men</u> take part in sports, too. _____

8. Jack wore a guard to protect his <u>teeth</u>. _____

9. A <u>child</u> can play sports at school. _____

10. <u>Geese</u> do not play sports. _____

Name _____ Date _____

Vowel Sound in *joy*

Spelling Words

Basic
1. joy
2. point
3. voice
4. join
5. oil
6. coin
7. noise
8. spoil
9. toy
10. joint
11. boy
12. soil
13. choice

Review
come
are

Challenge
poison
destroy

Use the Basic Words to complete the puzzle.

Across
1. a decision
3. to become a member
5. a sound
7. dirt
8. the tip of a pencil
10. to heat a liquid until it bubbles
11. great happiness

Down
1. a metal piece of money
2. a dark, slippery liquid
3. the place where two bones connect
4. what one uses to speak
6. to go bad
9. something to play with
10. a male child

Name _____ Date _____

Suffixes *-less*, *-ful*, *-ous*

In each sentence, circle the word with the suffix *-less*, *-ful*, or *-ous*. Then write the base word, the suffix, and the word meaning. Use context clues in the sentence to help you find the meaning.

1. Uncle Mario is a skillful carpenter who can build just about anything out of wood.

_____   _____   _____
    base word   **suffix**   **meaning**

2. Gloria was happy to hear that her trip to the dentist would be painless.

_____   _____   _____
    base word   **suffix**   **meaning**

3. My grandmother is an adventurous person who likes to see new places and try new things.

_____   _____   _____
    base word   **suffix**   **meaning**

4. It is hard to say no to our coach because he is such a powerful person.

_____   _____   _____
    base word   **suffix**   **meaning**

5. Our dog Red sometimes yelps in his sleep, but he had a dreamless nap today.

_____   _____   _____
    base word   **suffix**   **meaning**

Lesson 11
READER'S NOTEBOOK

**Technology Wins
the Game**

Grammar:
Spiral Review

Kinds of Verbs

- A word that tells what people or things do is a **verb**. Words that show action are **action verbs**.
- Some verbs do not show action. They are being **verbs**. The verbs *am*, *is*, *are*, *was*, and *were* are forms of the verb *be*. They tell what someone or something is or was.

    The players <u>jump</u>, and they <u>are</u> strong.

Identify the underlined verb in each sentence. Write *action* or *being* on the line.

1. Tammy <u>worked</u> hard for the race. _____

2. She <u>was</u> a weak runner. _____

3. Her coach <u>taught</u> her exercises. _____

Combine each pair of sentences. Use both verbs in the new sentence. Write the new sentence on the line.

4. Jena jumped four feet high. Jena landed in the foam pit.

_____

5. The team ran around the track. The team was soon tired.

_____

6. The coaches were impressed. The coaches were happy.

_____

Name _____ Date _____

Lesson 11
READER'S NOTEBOOK

Proofread for Spelling

Circle the ten misspelled Spelling Words in the following letter. Then write each word correctly.

**Technology Wins
the Game**
Spelling:
Vowel Sound in *joy*

Dear Louise,

    I hope that you are doing well. I wish that I could jion you this week at camp. Sadly, I've lost my voic, so Mom says I have to rest. Sitting inside while everyone else has fun definitely wouldn't be my choyce. Boiy, am I bored! I did get a cool new toi, though. It is a tiny robot that makes a weird noyse whenever you poiynt a light at it. I think Dad wants to destroiy it already. He thinks playing with it is like poyson to my brain and says I should read more books. He's probably right. Oh, I also got a neat old coyn from my grandfather. Anyway, write back when you can!

              Your friend,

              Albert

Spelling Words

Basic
1. joy
2. point
3. voice
4. join
5. oil
6. coin
7. noise
8. spoil
9. toy
10. joint
11. boy
12. soil
13. choice
14. boil

Review
come
are

Challenge
poison
destroy

1. _____ 6. _____

2. _____ 7. _____

3. _____ 8. _____

4. _____ 9. _____

5. _____ 10. _____

Name _____ Date _____

Lesson 11
READER'S NOTEBOOK

Technology Wins the Game
Grammar:
Connect to Writing

Connect to Writing

If a noun ends with a consonant and *y*, change the *y* to *i*, and add *-es* to form the plural.

Sometimes the spelling of a noun changes in a special way.

The spelling of some nouns does not change to form the plural.

Incorrectly Formed Plural	Correctly Formed Plural
cherry, cherrys	cherry, cherries
goose, gooses	goose, geese
deer, deers	deer, deer

Proofread the paragraph. Find five mistakes in the spelling of plural nouns. Write the corrected sentences on the lines below.

> The mans on the ski team learned a lot from the women. They showed them how to relax and go faster. They told storys about great women skiers.
> On top of the mountain, the skiers saw deers. They had to be careful not to run into them. Two women fell on the way down. Their familys were worried. But they were all right. Now they don't have any worrys.

1. _____

2. _____

3. _____

4. _____

5. _____

Name _____ Date _____

Lesson 12
READER'S NOTEBOOK

Tops and Bottoms
Phonics:
Homophones

Homophones

Read each sentence. Choose the missing word from the box. Write the word. Then reread the complete sentence.

chews	mail	heal
choose	cent	heel
male	sent	he'll

1. A stallion is a _____ horse.

2. I didn't have a _____ in my purse.

3. That wound should _____ in a few days.

4. Becky's shoe was worn down at the _____.

5. Ernesto always _____ his food slowly.

6. Ginger's uncle _____ her a birthday present.

7. Watch for an important letter in the _____.

8. It is hard to _____ between two of your favorite foods.

9. If the cat doesn't like his food, _____ complain.

Quotation Marks

- **Quotation marks** (" ") show dialogue, or the exact words a person or character says.
- Put quotation marks at the beginning and the end of a person or character's exact words.

> at the beginning
>
> Sherry said, "I am determined to grow flowers in my yard."
>
> at the end

Thinking Question
What are the exact words of the speaker?

Rewrite the sentences, adding quotation marks as needed.

1. Sherry said, This summer, I will start a garden.

   _____

2. Cindy asked, What plants will you grow?

   _____

3. Sherry replied, I was thinking of planting sunflower seeds.

   _____

4. Cindy exclaimed, I love sunflowers!

   _____

174

Capitalizing and Punctuating Quotations

- Always capitalize the first word of the speaker's exact words.

- If the quotation comes first, add a comma, question mark, or exclamation point inside the **quotation marks** at the end of the speaker's words and add a period at the end of the sentence.

- If the quotation comes last, add a comma at the end of the tag and a question mark, exclamation point, or period inside the quotation marks.

Thinking Questions
What are the first and last words of the speaker? Which end mark is correct for the quotation? Does the quotation begin or end the sentence?

Rewrite the sentences with correct capitalization and punctuation.

1. Sherry exclaimed "my flowers are growing so well"

   _____

2. Marco asked "what did you do to help them grow"

   _____

3. "my sister and I weeded and watered them every day" replied Sherry

   _____

   _____

4. "carrying water is hard work" exclaimed Sherry

   _____

Homophones

Write Basic Words to answer the following questions.

1. Which two words use the same vowel sound as *air*?

_____ , _____

2. Which two words use the same vowel sound as *ear*?

_____ , _____

3. Which two words use the same vowel sound as *burn*?

_____ , _____

4. Which two words use the same vowel sound as *once*?

_____ , _____

5. Which two words use the same vowel sound as *go*?

_____ , _____

6. Which two words use the same vowel sound as *in*?

_____ , _____

7. Which two words use the same vowel sound as *now*?

_____ , _____

Challenge: Write two sentences. Use one Challenge Word in each sentence.

1. _____

2. _____

Spelling Words

Basic
1. hole
2. whole
3. its
4. it's
5. hear
6. here
7. won
8. one
9. our
10. hour
11. their
12. there
13. fur
14. fir

Review
road
rode

Challenge
peace
piece

Focus Trait: Evidence
Details to Compare and Contrast

A compare-and-contrast paragraph tells how two or more things are alike and different. Good writers use to help them compare and contrast things.

Without details: Carrots and lettuce are different in color.

With details: Carrots are orange, but lettuce is green.

Use detail words to describe each vegetable.

Carrot	Beet
1.	
2.	

Use detail words from your list above to write one sentence comparing and one sentence contrasting the vegetables.

3. _____

4. _____

Pair/Share   Work with a partner to describe each vegetable. Then write a sentence comparing them and a sentence contrasting them.

Lettuce	Corn
5.	
6.	

7. _____

8. _____

Words Ending in -*er*, -*le*

Write a word from the box to complete each sentence
in the story. Then read the complete sentence.

bottle	ladle	table
dreamer	longer	teacher
kettle	sweeter	warmer

1. "Wake up, _____!" my mom calls every morning.

2. "Can't I sleep a little _____?" I always ask.

3. Soon I am in the kitchen, where it is _____
   and full of action.

4. The _____ is already set for breakfast.

5. I get the _____ of milk from the refrigerator.

6. In a few minutes the tea _____ whistles and
   the water is ready.

7. I love making Mom's tea for her. "Just a bit more honey,

   to make it _____," I say.

8. Then I watch as Dad puts a _____ full of
   oatmeal in my favorite bowl. Yum!

9. He wraps up a muffin, smiles, and winks. "Give this to

   your _____ before school today."

Name _____ Date _____

Lesson 12
READER'S NOTEBOOK

Tops and Bottoms
Independent Reading

Tops and Bottoms

Gardening Journal

Hi, I'm Hare! I am keeping a garden journal to record the planting and harvesting. Help me fill it in with information from the text.

Read page 434. How did I get started?

_____

_____

_____

Read page 435. How did I take care of the land?

_____

_____

_____

Read page 438. Tell about the harvest. What was clever about what I grew?

_____

_____

_____

Read pages 439–440. What was the next plan?

_____

_____

_____

_____

Read page 443. Why was Bear angry again?

_____

_____

_____

_____

Read pages 444–449. How did Bear think he would win this time?

_____

_____

_____

_____

Read page 450. What did Bear finally do?

_____

_____

_____

_____

Name _____ Date _____

Capitalizing and Punctuating Quotations

- Capitalize the first word of the speaker's exact words.
- If the quotation comes first, add a comma, question mark, or exclamation point inside the **quotation marks** at the end of the speaker's words and add a period at the end of the sentence.
- If the quotation comes last, add a comma at the end of the tag and a question mark, exclamation point, or period inside the quotation marks.

Write the sentences using correct capitalization and punctuation.

1. Jessie asked "where are they selling their tomatoes"

   _____

2. "They have a roadside stand" replied Manny.

   _____

3. "Do they also sell cucumbers" asked Jessie.

   _____

4. "I'm not sure" Manny said.

   _____

5. Manny said "the stand is past this farm"

   _____

6. "They do have cucumbers" Jessie exclaimed.

   _____

Name _____ Date _____

Lesson 12
READER'S NOTEBOOK

Tops and Bottoms
Spelling:
Homophones

Who Am I?

Read each clue. Then write the correct word on the line.

1. Every day has 24 of me. _____

2. Wolves and bears wear me. _____

3. If you fall into me you might get hurt.

   _____

4. I am all, not just part. _____

5. I am first! _____

6. I have needles instead of leaves. _____

7. I am something people do with their ears.

   _____

8. I am something a team did. _____

Challenge: Explain the meanings of *peace* and *piece*.

_____

_____

Spelling Words

Basic
1. hole
2. whole
3. its
4. it's
5. hear
6. here
7. won
8. one
9. our
10. hour
11. their
12. there
13. fur
14. fir

Review
road
rode

Challenge
peace
piece

Name _____ Date _____

Lesson 12
READER'S NOTEBOOK

Tops and Bottoms
Vocabulary Strategies:
Idioms

Idioms

Read the web below. Write the meaning of each idiom. (You may find the meanings by looking up *head* in the dictionary.)

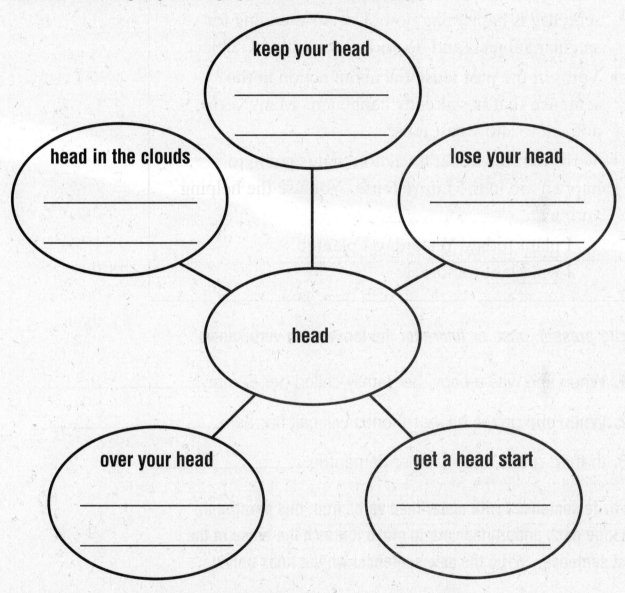

Choose one idiom from above and write two sentences. In the first sentence, write the meaning of the idiom. In the second sentence, replace the meaning with the idiom.

1. _____

2. _____

Verb Tenses

- Verbs in the **present tense** tell that the action in the sentence is happening now. Use an -s ending for singular subjects and no ending for a plural subject.
- Verbs in the **past tense** tell about action in the sentence that has already happened. Many verbs add -ed to show past tense.
- Verbs that tell about an action that is going to happen are in the **future tense**. You use the helping verb *will*.

  I <u>plant</u> today. Yesterday, I <u>planted</u>.
  I <u>will plant</u> tomorrow.

Write *present*, *past*, or *future* for the tense each verb shows.

1. When she was a baby, her family called her Sammy. _____

2. When she grows up, her friends will call her Sam. _____

3. In third grade, they call her Samantha. _____

Rewrite sentences with underlined verbs from this paragraph. Change each underlined verb to make it match the tense of the first sentence. Write the new sentences on the lines below.

Our dog, Yappy, ran into the street. My brother <u>calls</u> to him very loudly. Yappy <u>will stop</u> for my brother.

4. _____

5. _____

Proofreading for Spelling

Find the misspelled words and circle them. Then write each word correctly.

Dear Pat,

    I'm writing this in the shade of a big fur tree. Its soft needles cover the ground like a blanket. Its a quiet summer day in the city's biggest park. All around, their is a feeling of piece and restfulness. My dog, Corvo, lies lazily in the hot sun. I'll bet his fir makes him hot on this summer day. I pick up a peace of paper that someone has left on the ground. Let's keep the city clean! I've been hear an our, and I could stay all day. I can hardly here the traffic. The cars with there noise seem far away. I like writing letters, but I wish you were here!

                Your friend,

                Chris

Spelling Words

Basic
1. hole
2. whole
3. its
4. it's
5. hear
6. here
7. won
8. one
9. our
10. hour
11. their
12. there
13. fur
14. fir

Review
road
rode

Challenge
peace
piece

1. _____   6. _____

2. _____   7. _____

3. _____   8. _____

4. _____   9. _____

5. _____   10. _____

Connect to Writing

Use quotation marks (" ") to show the exact words someone says. A quotation may come before or after the tag.

Before the Tag	After the Tag
"I'll help make dinner," Ralph said.	Ralph said, "I'll help make dinner."
"What would you like to eat?" Pete asked.	Pete asked, "What would you like to eat?"

Rewrite the sentences, adding quotation marks and commas as needed.

1. I would like roasted vegetables Ralph replied.

_____

2. Pete said I have carrots.

_____

3. Would you like carrots Pete asked.

_____

4. I love carrots! Ralph exclaimed.

_____

5. They are one of my favorites said Pete.

_____

Contractions with *n't*, *'d*, *'ve*

Read each sentence. Choose the missing word
from the box. Write the word. Then reread the complete sentence.

aren't	couldn't	should've
they'd	you'd	haven't
I've	we've	I'd

1. If I ever had to sleep in the woods,

   _____ bring lots of bug spray.

2. I tried to open the jar, but I _____ because
   the lid was on too tight.

3. If you saw the movie, _____ love it as much
   as I did.

4. My parents _____ too strict, but they do
   have some rules.

5. Personally, _____ always admired Ben
   Franklin.

6. We haven't seen the movie, but _____
   both read the book.

7. "I _____ known that you were behind all of
   this," said the hero to the villain.

8. Why are you serving us dessert when we _____
   eaten dinner yet?

9. If our friends saw us, _____ be really surprised.

Subject-Verb Agreement

- A **verb** that tells about an action that is happening now is in the present tense. Verbs in the present tense have two forms. The correct form to use depends on the **subject** of the sentence.
- Except for *I*, add *-s* to the verb when the noun in the subject is singular. Do not add *-s* to the verb when the noun in the subject is plural.

> The word *Cherokee* <u>means</u> "people who live in the mountains."
>
> The Cherokee now <u>live</u> mostly in Oklahoma and North Carolina.

Thinking Question
Is the noun in the subject singular or plural?

Underline the correct present-tense verb in parentheses. Then write each sentence correctly.

1. People (hear, hears) the Cherokee language.

   _____

2. Fur trader Abraham Wood (send, sends) two men.

   _____

3. The program about the Cherokee (begins, begin) at 7:00.

   _____

4. The Cherokee (moves, move) to the west in the 1880s.

   _____

Subject-Verb Agreement

- Some **verbs** end with -es instead of -s. Add -es to verbs that end with s, sh, ch, or x when they are used with a singular noun in the **subject**. Do not add -es when the noun in the subject is plural.

- Some verbs end with a consonant and y. Change the y to i, and add -es when you use this kind of verb with a singular noun.

  Thinking Question
  Does the verb end in s, sh, ch, x, *or a consonant and* y?

  The town searches for a new music director.
  A singer worries it will not happen.

- The verb *search* adds -es. The verb *worry* changes the y to i and adds -es.

Underline the correct present-tense verb in parentheses. Then write each sentence correctly.

1. A newspaper writer (asks, askes) for a new music director.

_____

2. A town citizen (watchs, watches) for a new music director.

_____

3. A woman who knows music (hurrys, hurries) into town.

_____

4. She (trys, tries) to get everyone to sing well together.

_____

Name _____ Date _____

Contractions

Write each Basic Word under the correct heading.

Contractions combining a base word and *not*	Contractions combining a base word and *is*, *us*, or *has*
_____	_____
_____	_____
_____	_____
_____	_____
_____	_____
_____	_____

Contractions combining a base word and *are*	Contractions combining a base word and *had* or *would*
_____	_____
_____	_____
_____	_____

Challenge: Add the Challenge Words to your Word Sort.

Spelling Words

Basic
1. I'd
2. he's
3. haven't
4. doesn't
5. let's
6. there's
7. wouldn't
8. what's
9. she's
10. aren't
11. hasn't
12. couldn't
13. he'd
14. they're

Review
can't
isn't

Challenge
we're
weren't

Yonder Mountain
Writing: Informative Writing

Focus Trait: Organization
Group Related Information

An informative paragraph gives facts and details about a topic. When you write an informative paragraph, group related information together.

Read pages 479–480 of *Yonder Mountain*. **Write facts and details about Gray Wolf in the web.**

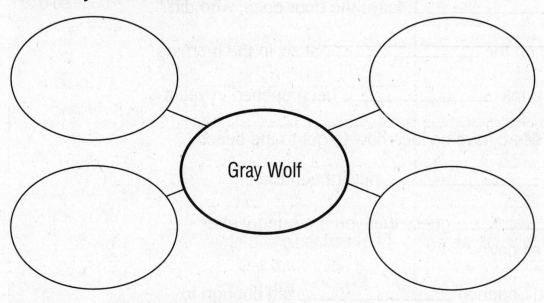

Gray Wolf

Pair/Share **Work with a partner to write sentences that group the information in the web.**

_____

_____

_____

_____

_____

Name _____ Date _____

Lesson 13
READER'S NOTEBOOK

Yonder Mountain:
A Cherokee Legend
Phonics:
Cumulative Review

Cumulative Review

**Write a word from the box to complete each sentence.
Then read the sentence.**

road	they've	we've
you'd	I'd	rode
aren't	hasn't	didn't

1. If you _____ leave the door open, who did?

2. We were on the _____ at six in the morning.

3. This old trunk _____ been opened in years.

4. Eric and Marc have no idea how to get to the beach

because _____ never been there.

5. _____ guess that you are hungry after

working all day.

6. Carla and Shannon _____ old enough to

stay up so late.

7. Dee was excited to tell her friends how she

_____ a horse on vacation.

8. If _____ just listen more, and talk less, you

could learn a lot.

9. My cousin pulled me outside, saying, "_____

got to leave now!"

Yonder Mountain

A Scene from Yonder Mountain

You are going to tell the story of Yonder Mountain as a
play. Fill in the different parts with details from the story.

Read pages 473–475. Use what you read on these pages to write
a script for Chief Sky. Help him tell the audience how the three
young men are alike. What do they want? What do they do?

Chief Sky: _____

_____

_____

Read pages 476–480. Use these pages to help Black Bear
and Gray Wolf tell the audience about their adventures.

Black Bear: _____

_____

_____

Gray Wolf: _____

_____

_____

_____

Read pages 481–484. Use what you read on these pages to write the script for Soaring Eagle. He will tell the audience about his journey up the mountain.

Soaring Eagle: _____

_____

_____

_____

Read pages 485–487. Why did Chief Sky choose Soaring Eagle to be the new chief? Write a script for Chief Sky. He will tell the audience why he chose Soaring Eagle.

Chief Sky: _____

_____

_____

_____

_____

Lesson 13
READER'S NOTEBOOK

**Yonder Mountain:
A Cherokee Legend**
Grammar:
Subject-Verb Agreement

Subject-Verb Agreement

The subject of each sentence is underlined. Write the correct form of the verb in parentheses to complete each sentence.

1. A <u>climber</u> _____ for a way to the top. (search)

2. Two strong <u>men</u> _____ themselves up the cliffs. (pull)

3. A <u>woman</u> _____ her ropes to be safe. (fix)

4. One <u>person</u> _____ another as they climb. (pass)

5. <u>Friends</u> _____ someone who is tired. (help)

6. Some <u>boys</u> _____ to see who can be first to the top. (race)

7. A <u>bird</u> _____ up to the highest point. (fly)

8. One <u>group</u> _____ a deep valley on the way. (cross)

9. One tired <u>person</u> _____ on the way up. (slip)

10. <u>I</u> _____ the top of the mountain first. (reach)

Name _____ Date _____

Contractions

Write the Spelling Word that is a contraction of each word
pair below.

1. have not _____

2. what is _____

3. let us _____

4. he had _____

5. could not _____

6. there is _____

7. are not _____

8. she is _____

9. they are _____

10. does not _____

11. I had _____

12. would not _____

13. he is _____

14. has not _____

Spelling Words

Basic
1. I'd
2. he's
3. haven't
4. doesn't
5. let's
6. there's
7. wouldn't
8. what's
9. she's
10. aren't
11. hasn't
12. couldn't
13. he'd
14. they're

Review
can't
isn't

Challenge
we're
weren't

Homophones and Homographs

Read the following paragraph. Proofread it to find mistakes with homophones. Write the wrong homophone and the correct homophone on the lines.

My grandmother and I walked to the park. On our weigh, we passed a fruit stand.

"Mind if we peak at your selection?" my grandmother asked.

"Go ahead!" the fruit vendor said. "I have all kinds of fresh fruits write here! Here, have this red pare," he added. "It's perfectly ripe."

"Thanks," my grandmother said. "I almost mist that one!"

1. _____

2. _____

3. _____

4. _____

5. _____

Choose a pair of homophones. Write a sentence that shows the meaning of each word.

_____

_____

Name _____ Date _____

Lesson 13
READER'S NOTEBOOK

**Yonder Mountain:
A Cherokee Legend**
Grammar:
Spiral Review

Writing Quotations

- Show dialogue by putting quotation marks (" ") at the beginning and the end of a speaker's exact words.

    She asked, "Are you climbing?"

- Place a comma after *said* or *asked*. Use a capital letter for the first word of the quotation and an end mark inside the quotation marks.

    He said, "Give it to me."

    "We're finally home!" Kim shouted.

Write each sentence correctly by adding quotation marks.

1. The teacher said, Hillary climbed the tallest mountain.

    _____

2. She asked, What is the tallest mountain called?

    _____

3. He said, It is named Mount Everest.

    _____

Write each sentence correctly. Use quotation marks, correct capitalization, end marks, and punctuation.

4. The teacher asked would you like to climb a mountain

    _____

5. The girl said climbing Mount Everest would be exciting

    _____

Name _____ Date _____

Proofreading

Circle the ten misspelled Spelling Words in the following story. Then write each word correctly.

Spelling Words

Basic

1. I'd
2. he's
3. haven't
4. doesn't
5. let's
6. there's
7. wouldn't
8. what's
9. she's
10. aren't
11. hasn't
12. couldn't
13. he'd
14. they're

Review

can't
isn't

Challenge

we're
weren't

My Relatives

My aunt and uncle are very different from a lot of people. Hes a clown in a circus, and she works as a stuntwoman. Theyr'e always doing crazy stuff. For example, my aunt has'nt cut her hair in fifteen years. I know I couln'ot go six months without getting a haircut. Then theres the house where they live. Lets' just say that it is unique. For starters, it do'snt have any corners. You wouldnt believe how odd it looks. When we stay with them, I feel like wer'e living in a donut! If they were'nt so nice, I might think that there was actually something wrong with them.

1. _____   6. _____

2. _____   7. _____

3. _____   8. _____

4. _____   9. _____

5. _____   10. _____

Name _____ Date _____

Lesson 13
READER'S NOTEBOOK

**Yonder Mountain:
A Cherokee Legend**
Grammar:
Connect to Writing

Connect to Writing

Proofreading is important to make writing correct and clear to the reader. Pay attention to endings of verbs as you proofread.

Singular Subject	Plural Subject
The Native American chief leads.	Chiefs lead.
He mixes an herb as medicine.	They mix herbs as medicine.
The chief thinks about his people.	Chiefs think about their people.
He works for a solution.	They work for a solution.

Proofread the paragraph. Find and underline five errors with the spelling of present tense verbs. Write the corrected sentences.

> The chief of the Native American group knows it is time to move. The land lack the food needed for their people. It is time to go south. The women carries the things they want to bring. Some men on horses searches for a place to stay. They find a wonderful place by the river. The children rushes to get there first. Everyone enjoys the new area. A horse splash through the river water. Everyone smiles for the first time in a long time.

1. _____

2. _____

3. _____

4. _____

5. _____

Words with *ar, or, ore*

Read each sentence. Choose the missing word from the box. Write the word. Then reread the sentence.

Mars	morning	cart
chores	parking	largest
artistic	explore	parlor

1. This tree is the _____ tree on the street.

2. "Have a seat in the _____," said the butler to the guest.

3. The bold scientists planned to _____ the bottom of the ocean.

4. The driver looked for a _____ space for five minutes.

5. Put your groceries into the _____.

6. My favorite time of day is _____.

7. Painting, singing, and dancing are _____ hobbies.

8. I wish I could fly to the planet _____.

9. Taking out the trash and making my bed are on my list of

_____.

Pronoun-Verb Agreement

- Verbs show action in sentences and when that action happens. **Verbs** that tell about actions that are happening now are in the present tense.
- You add *-s* or *-es* to the verb when the **pronoun** in the **subject** is *he*, *she*, or *it*.
- You do not add *-s* or *-es* to the verb when the pronoun in the subject is *I*, *you*, *we*, or *they*.

    She <u>barks</u> very loudly.

    They <u>bark</u> even more loudly.

Thinking Question
Does the subject pronoun refer just to one person or does it refer either to me or to more than one person?

Underline the present-tense verb in parentheses that agrees with the subject pronoun. Then write each sentence correctly.

1. You (find, finds) dogs of all different types.

_____

2. He (choose, chooses) the ones that are the best.

_____

3. It (seem, seems) that you know dogs well.

_____

4. We (feel, feels) that you should choose the dogs.

_____

5. They (want, wants) to pick out some dogs, too.

_____

When to Add -*es*, -*ies*

- Most **verbs** in the present end with -*s* when the **pronoun** in the **subject** is *he*, *she*, or *it*. Add -*es* to verbs that end in -*s*, -*sh*, -*ch*, or -*x*.
- Do not add -*s* or -*es* to verbs when the pronoun in the subject is *I*, *you*, *we*, or *they*.
- Some verbs end with a consonant and *y*. Change the *y* to *i* and add -*es* when the pronoun in the subject is *he*, *she*, or *it*.
- You do not change the *y* to *i* and add -*es* when the pronoun in the subject is *I*, *you*, *we*, or *they*.

Thinking Question
Does the verb end in s, sh, ch, x or with a consonant and y, and what is the pronoun in the subject?

Underline the present-tense verb in parentheses that agrees with the subject pronoun. Then write each sentence correctly.

1. You (push, pushes) the cart filled with hay out to the fields.

_____

2. It (pass, passes) over the old bridge.

_____

3. We (guess, guesses) when you will reach the horses.

_____

4. They (march, marches) across the hills to the food.

_____

Words with Vowel + /r/ Sounds

Write the correct Basic Words in each box.

Write the words that contain the vowel + r sound in *far*.	Write the words that contain the vowel + r sound in *or*.
_____	_____
_____	_____
_____	_____
_____	_____
_____	_____
	_____
	_____
	_____

Challenge

1. Does *partner* contain the vowel sound in *far* or the vowel sound in *or*? _____

2. Does *fortune* contain the vowel sound in *far* or the vowel sound in *or*? _____

Spelling Words

Basic
1. horse
2. mark
3. storm
4. market
5. acorn
6. artist
7. March
8. north
9. barking
10. stork
11. thorn
12. forest
13. chore
14. restore

Review
dark
story

Challenge
partner
fortune

Focus Trait: Purpose
Choosing a Topic

An explanatory essay uses ideas, facts, and details to explain a topic to readers. Good writers ask, *What is my purpose for writing? What topic am I interested in? What ideas do I have about the topic? How can I use facts and details to explain the topic clearly?*

Read the information in the chart. Look at the topics and the author's purpose. Which topic interests you the most? Circle it.

Topics	Author's Purpose
how dogs help people how monkeys help people how horses help people how dolphins help people	to explain a topic to readers

Tell why you chose the topic. Also list one or two ideas that you have about the topic.

_____

_____

_____

_____

Name _____ Date _____

Lesson 14
READER'S NOTEBOOK

Aero and Officer Mike
Phonics:
Cumulative Review

Cumulative Review

Write words from the box to complete the lines of the poem.

arm	garden	I'd	shark	storm
bored	harm	I've	shore	thorns

What Didn't Go Wrong Today?

I worked in my_____, but I soon came to _____.

The sharp _____ of a rose badly scratched up

   my _____!

So I went to the _____ for a swim and some sun,

Until a _____ showed its fin and scared everyone!

Then _____ just reached the woods, the shade of tall trees,

When a dark _____ filled the sky and rained on the seas!

Now _____ come home sad, with nothing to do.

If you are _____, too, may I come play with you?

Aero and Officer Mike

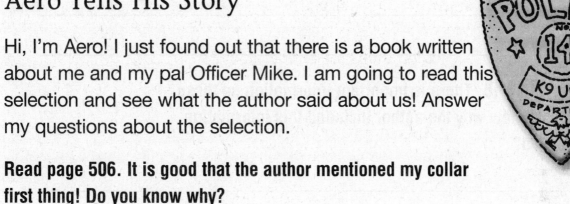

Aero Tells His Story

Hi, I'm Aero! I just found out that there is a book written about me and my pal Officer Mike. I am going to read this selection and see what the author said about us! Answer my questions about the selection.

Read page 506. It is good that the author mentioned my collar first thing! Do you know why?

_____

_____

Read pages 508–509. The author mentioned Officer Mike's police car. Why do you think the car is important?

_____

_____

Read pages 510–511. I love playing ball with Mike! I also listen to Mike when he talks to me. Can you guess why?

_____

_____

Read page 512. I remember that training! I still don't really like looking at those pictures. What can you tell about the training from looking at the pictures? How did I feel about it?

_____

_____

_____

Read pages 516–518. There is important information on these pages. Do you know why the author included this information in this selection?

_____

_____

_____

Read pages 519–521. I thought this was a really good book! It explained a lot about Officer Mike and me! Now you tell me what you thought of this selection. Did you like it? Why or why not?

_____

_____

_____

Pronoun-Verb Agreement

**Write the present-tense form of the verb in parentheses
that agrees with the subject pronoun.**

1. My dogs _____ all day. (sleep)

2. They _____ my smell and trust me. (learn)

3. He _____ other ways to get close to his dogs. (use)

4. She _____ them right out of her hand. (feed)

5. You _____ here and watch us do it. (sit)

6. The dogs _____ as they play in the rain. (splash)

7. It _____ your attention when you see it. (catch)

8. He _____ a special blend of pet food. (mix)

9. One _____ a ball that he throws. (catch)

10. They _____ the different ways to train pets. (study)

Words with Vowel + /r/ Sounds

Aero and Officer Mike
Spelling:
Vowel + /r/ Sounds

Write eight words that are names for people, places, or things.

_____

_____

_____

_____

_____

_____

_____

Challenge

1. A person you work with is your _____.

2. If you make a lot of money, you make a

_____.

Name _____ Date _____

Lesson 14
READER'S NOTEBOOK

Aero and Officer Mike
Vocabulary Strategies:
Prefixes *in-*, *im-*

Prefixes *in-*, im-

Read each base word. Add the prefix shown and write
a new word and its meaning.

Base Word	Prefix	New Word	Meaning
active	in		
visible	in		
definite	in		
patient	im		
perfect	im		
measurable	im		

Now write a sentence for each word above with a prefix. Make
sure your sentence shows the word's meaning.

1. _____

2. _____

3. _____

4. _____

5. _____

6. _____

Name _____ Date _____

Lesson 14
READER'S NOTEBOOK

Aero and Officer Mike
Grammar:
Spiral Review

Subjects and Predicates

- The subject of a sentence tells whom or what the sentence is about.
- The predicate of a sentence tells what the subject is, was, or will be, or what the subject is, was, or will be doing.

    The sheep ate grass in the valley.

    An old wolf watched them from the bushes.

Write the subject of each sentence on the line.

1. The old gray coyote came out of the hills. _____

2. This smart animal will eat almost anything. _____

3. His little pups hide right behind him. _____

4. These sweet babies are hungry and tired. _____

Write the predicate of each sentence on the line.

5. Three fat sheep walk away from the others. _____

6. A big blue truck drives by them. _____

7. A man with boots grabs the sheep. _____

8. The coyote finds food for the pups. _____

Name _____ Date _____

Lesson 14
READER'S NOTEBOOK

Aero and Officer Mike
Spelling:
Vowel + /r/ Sounds

Words with Vowel + /r/ Sounds

Find the misspelled words and circle them. Then write each word correctly.

An ortist was traveling through a deep, dark farest. He carried his paints and brushes in a bag that hung from his back. His harse was white, just like a blank canvas. He was riding to the morket, a day's ride to the narth, to sell his pictures. Suddenly, huge gray clouds moved overhead. A storem was coming! The wind rose, and an acarn fell from a tree, hitting the man on the head. A sharp tharn from a bush scratched his hand. A big white stark flapped its wings as it flew toward its nest. Then the traveler heard the barrking of wild dogs in the distance. "Don't worry," he told his horse. "They're afraid of thunder and lightning."

Spelling Words

Basic
1. horse
2. mark
3. storm
4. market
5. acorn
6. artist
7. March
8. north
9. barking
10. stork
11. thorn
12. forest
13. chore
14. restore

Review
dark
story

Challenge
partner
fortune

1. _____   6. _____

2. _____   7. _____

3. _____   8. _____

4. _____   9. _____

5. _____   10. _____

Connect to Writing

Combining two sentences that have the same noun in the subject makes your writing smoother and easier to read. Remember to use a comma and the word *and*.

Same Noun in the Subject	Pronoun Replacing Noun in the Subject
These dogs are for sports. These dogs make great pets.	These dogs are for sports, and they make great pets.
Border collies are herding dogs. Border collies are very smart.	Border collies are herding dogs, and they are very smart.

Combine each pair of sentences. Change each underlined subject to a pronoun. Write the new sentence.

1. Maltese dogs are friendly. <u>Maltese dogs</u> make good pets.

   _____

2. My male Great Dane is very gentle. <u>My male Great Dane</u> stands very tall.

   _____

3. Your female collie tends sheep. <u>Your female collie</u> gets burrs in her fur.

   _____

4. The people who breed dogs work very hard. <u>The people who breed dogs</u> love animals.

   _____

5. My family and I look for the perfect dog. <u>My family and I</u> find a funny one we love.

   _____

Name _____ Date _____

Lesson 15
READER'S NOTEBOOK

Words with *er, ir, ur, or*

The Extra-good Sunday
Phonics:
Words with *er, ir, ur, or*

Read each sentence. Choose the missing word from the box.
Write the word. Then reread the complete sentence.

curb	nerve	curves
worker	furry	birth
thirty	germs	

1. The road _____ up ahead, so be ready to turn.

2. Having hair on the furniture is one of the problems with having a

_____ dog.

3. I knew you wouldn't have the _____ to stand up to your
big brother.

4. As Danielle crossed the street, she tripped on the _____ and
hurt her ankle.

5. Adam does well in school because he is a hard _____.

6. The zoo announced the _____ of a baby panther last week.

7. Mr. Perkins has _____ students in his classroom.

8. Colds and the flu are caused by _____.

Verbs in the Past

- Most verbs show **past tense** by adding -*ed*.
- Some verbs end with *e*. Drop the *e* and add -*ed*.
    They <u>allowed</u> us to cook alone.
    He <u>needed</u> eggs for the recipe.
    Evan's parents <u>liked</u> our cooking.

Thinking Question
Can I add -ed to the verb to show past tense? Does the verb end in e?

Write each sentence using the correct past tense of the verb in parentheses.

1. Evan _____ his parents to send him to cooking school. (want)

   _____

2. We _____ to answer a newspaper ad for a school. (decide)

   _____

3. Many cooking students _____ there. (work)

   _____

4. Evan and I _____ that they would like our letter. (hope)

   _____

5. We _____ the school with the good work we did. (surprise)

   _____

Verbs in the Present

- Add -s to most **present tense** verbs when the noun in the subject is singular. For most verbs that end in y, change the y to i and add -es.
- Do not add -s to the verb when the noun in the subject is plural.
- Do not add -s to the verb when the subject is I or you.

> Mario <u>eats</u> in the kitchen. He <u>studies</u> alone.
>
> We <u>eat</u> together. We <u>study</u> together.
>
> I <u>eat</u> alone. I <u>study</u> with my sister.

Thinking Questions
Is the noun in the subject singular or plural? Is the noun I or you? Does the verb end in y?

Write each sentence, using the correct present tense of the verb in parentheses.

1. Uncle Raul _____ a cutting board. (use)

   _____

2. He _____ his tea while we slice onions. (sip)

   _____

3. I _____ when I slice onions. (cry)

   _____

4. Even my dad _____ when he slices onions. (cry)

   _____

Vowel + /r/ Sound in *nurse*

Write each Basic Word under the correct heading.

Words with the vowel + /r/ sound in *nurse* spelled *ur*	Words with the vowel + /r/ sound in *nurse* spelled *ir*
_____	_____
_____	_____
_____	_____
_____	_____
_____	_____

Words with the vowel + /r/ sound in *nurse* spelled *or*	Words with the vowel + /r/ sound in *nurse* spelled *er*
_____	_____
_____	_____

Spelling Words

Basic
1. nurse
2. work
3. shirt
4. hurt
5. first
6. word
7. serve
8. curly
9. dirt
10. third
11. worry
12. turn
13. stir
14. firm

Review
her
girl

Challenge
perfect
hamburger

Challenge: Which Challenge Word can only be placed in the last

box? _____

Which Challenge Word can be placed in both the first and the last

box? _____

Focus Trait: Elaboration
Using Formal Language

Writers change their voice, or how they use their words and language, based on the purpose of their writing. For example, they use formal language with an explanatory essay to clearly state facts, definitions, and details.

For example:

Dolphins live in the ocean in groups called <u>pods</u>. They are <u>highly intelligent</u> <u>mammals</u> that <u>communicate</u> through sound, vision, touch, and taste.

The sentences below are written using informal language.
Rewrite them using formal language.

1. Tiny monkeys are so cute, and they help people, too!

   _____

2. That police officer is riding a cool bike. He is in a pretty big park.

   _____

   _____

3. I think horses work too hard. They chase cows and carry around people and stuff.

   _____

   _____

4. There's a brush fire! You'd better call 911!

   _____

   _____

Name _____ Date _____

Cumulative Review

Write a word from the box to complete each sentence. Then read the sentence.

certainly	herd	working
firmly	turning	burger
spark	report	before

1. This restaurant is known for having a great

_____ and tasty fries.

2. I love to help cook dinner. I think I'm _____
into a chef!

3. Damon gave a very interesting _____ about
the rain forests.

4. I _____ don't want to spend all weekend
studying.

5. The forest fire began with just a single _____.

6. Nicole was being silly when she said that she always ate

lunch _____ breakfast.

7. Frank held the ball _____ as he ran.

8. The cowboys rounded up the _____ of
cattle.

9. Because the dryer is not _____, my clothes
are still wet.

Reader's Guide

The Extra-good Sunday

Cooking with Beezus and Ramona

Hi, I am Todd Allen, host of *Cooking at Home!* Beezus and Ramona created a delicious chicken dish for dinner. We are going to find out how they made it!

Read pages 543–544 to answer Todd's questions.

Todd Allen: Ramona, you had to cook dinner one night for the family. How did you feel about that?

Ramona: _____

_____

Read page 545 to answer Todd's question.

Todd Allen: Beezus, you wanted to make something awful! Why? What made you change your mind?

Beezus: _____

_____

_____

Read pages 546–549 to answer to the next question.

Todd Allen: How did you come up with your special dish?

Ramona: _____

_____

_____

Read pages 550–552. Use these pages to help Beezus talk about what happened next.

Todd Allen: Beezus, how did you feel about the dinner you were making? Was Ramona helping?

Beezus: _____

_____

_____

Read page 554. Use this page to help the girls talk about serving the dinner and about their parents' reaction.

Todd Allen: All right, Ramona. Let's see this famous chicken dish. Mmm, it looks good! How did you feel when you brought it out to the table?

Ramona: _____

_____

Read pages 555–557. What did Ramona think?

Todd Allen: Tell me, Ramona, what was the best part of making dinner?

Ramona: _____

_____

Name _____ Date _____

Lesson 15
READER'S NOTEBOOK

The Extra-good Sunday
Grammar:
Verb Tenses

Verbs in the Future

> - A verb that tells about an action that will happen is in the **future tense**.
> - Add the word *will* before a verb to form the future tense.
>
>   I <u>will cook</u> the food.
>   My family <u>will eat</u> the food.

Write each sentence, using the correct future tense of the verb in parentheses.

1. Theo _____ the recipe cards. (study)

_____

2. He _____ which recipe to make. (decide)

_____

3. Doug _____ the chicken. (fry)

_____

4. Both boys _____ the sauce. (taste)

_____

5. The younger kids _____ the table. (set)

_____

6. Theo _____ the meal. (serve)

_____

Vowel + /r/ Sound in *nurse*

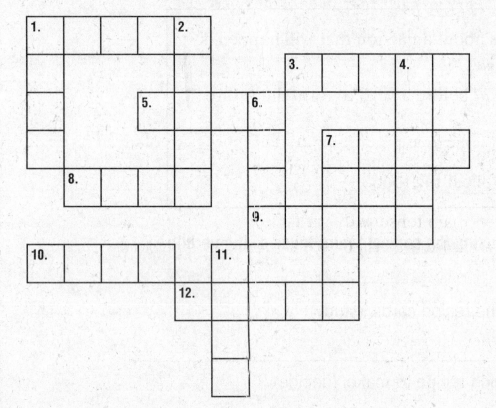

Spelling Words

Basic
1. nurse
2. work
3. shirt
4. hurt
5. first
6. word
7. serve
8. curly
9. dirt
10. third
11. worry
12. turn
13. stir
14. firm

Review
her
girl

Challenge
perfect
hamburger

Use the Basic Words to complete the puzzle.

Across

1. Item of clothing
3. Comes before "second"
5. Soil
7. The opposite of play
8. "Please" is the magic _____.
9. A hospital worker
10. Not soft
12. The opposite of straight

Down

1. To mix
2. Comes after "second"
4. To present or give
6. Move a car right or left
7. Be concerned
11. Injured

Name _____ Date _____

Lesson 15
READER'S NOTEBOOK

The Extra-good Sunday
Vocabulary Strategies:
Using a Thesaurus

Using a Thesaurus

Read the book review. Look up each underlined word in a thesaurus. Write a synonym for each word.

If you haven't already, you'll want to meet Ramona Quimby. The latest adventures of this special girl appear in *Ramona Quimby, Age 8*. With her father in college and her mother back at work, Ramona has to resolve some things for herself. How will she handle her annoying young neighbor? Will her parents be cross with her when she makes a mess? Will things remain tense with Yard Ape?

There is a reason why Beverly Cleary's books remain some of America's favorites after so many years.

1. _____

2. _____

3. _____

4. _____

5. _____

6. _____

Write two sentences that could be in your own review of *The Extra-good Sunday*. Choose a word in each sentence to look up in a thesaurus and underline it. Write a synonym for that word.

7. _____

8. _____

Kinds of Pronouns

- A **pronoun** is a word that can take the place of one or more nouns in a sentence. The pronouns *I, you, he, she, it, we,* and *they* are subject pronouns. Pronouns can be singular or plural.
- The words *me, you, him, her, it, us,* and *them* are object pronouns. Object pronouns follow action verbs and words like *to, for, at, of,* and *with.*

  Claude did not understand his parents.

  He did not understand them.

Write each sentence. Replace the underlined word or words with a subject or object pronoun.

1. Claude thinks his parents are good people.

   _____

2. Claude shows respect to his parents.

   _____

Replace the repeated noun in these sentences with a pronoun. Write the new sentences on the lines.

3. Claude loves to eat. Claude enjoys eating with his family.

   _____

4. Claude loves his friends. His friends see him every day.

   _____

Name _____ Date _____

Proofread for Spelling

**Circle the ten misspelled Spelling Words in this diary entry.
Then write each word correctly.**

> June 2nd
>
> Today was the purfect day. Dad decided to
> take a day off from wirk, and we went to the
> baseball game. Our seats were on the ferst base
> side of the field. The grass looked so green, and
> the durt on the infield looked so soft. As we sat
> down, Dad smiled and asked if my hair was getting
> more cirly. Before I could say a wurd, I saw my
> favorite player. He is the therd baseman, and he
> wears number 20 on his shurt. That's my favorite
> number, too! The last time we came to a game, he
> was hirt, but he was healthy today. Dad ordered
> me a hambirgur, and we settled in to watch a great
> game.

Spelling Words

Basic
1. nurse
2. work
3. shirt
4. hurt
5. first
6. word
7. serve
8. curly
9. dirt
10. third
11. worry
12. turn
13. stir
14. firm

Review
her
girl

Challenge
perfect
hamburger

1. _____   6. _____

2. _____   7. _____

3. _____   8. _____

4. _____   9. _____

5. _____   10. _____

Connect to Writing

Using incorrect verb tenses in your writing can confuse
the reader. Use the correct verb tense to show when actions
happen. Remember to use the correct verb endings or the
word *will* before the verb.

Present Tense	Past Tense	Future Tense
I talk.	I talked.	I will talk.
She talks.	She talked.	She will talk.
They talk.	They talked.	They will talk.

Choose the correct tense for each sentence. Write the verb.

1. The family (cooked, will cook) breakfast together. (future tense)

_____

2. Dad (mixes, mixed) the pancake batter in a bowl. (past tense)

_____

3. Harry (pours, will pour) the batter in the pan. (present tense)

_____

4. When the pancakes are ready, Harry (flipped, will flip) them. (future tense)

_____

5. Mom, Dad, and Harry (enjoy, will enjoy) their breakfast. (present tense)

_____

Reading and Writing Glossary

Use this glossary to help you remember and use words that you are learning about reading and writing.

A

abstract noun A noun that names an idea, a feeling, or a quality. Abstract nouns are things that people cannot see, hear, taste, smell, or touch.

action verb A verb that tells what people or things do.

adjective A word that describes a noun. Adjectives may also be used to compare nouns.

adverb A word that describes a verb, adjective, or other adverb. Adverbs may tell how, when, or where an action takes place.

analogy A kind of comparison in which one pair of words is compared to another. Each pair relates by definition, meaning, or characteristics.

analyze To look at or study carefully.

antecedent The noun that a pronoun replaces.

antonym A word that has the opposite, or nearly the opposite, meaning than another word.

article A word, such as *a*, *an*, or *the*, that comes before a noun. Articles tell which noun.

author's purpose The reason an author has for writing.

B

base word A word to which endings, prefixes, and suffixes can be added.

biography A story about the events in a person's life told in time order.

C

··

caption Text that explains a photo or picture.

cause An event that makes something else happen.

character A person in a story.

chart A drawing that lists information in a way that makes it clear and easy to understand.

clarify To make clear.

comma Punctuation mark that tells a reader where to pause. A comma can also help to make a sentence's meaning more clear.

command A type of sentence that gives an order. A command may end with a period (.) or an exclamation mark (!).

common noun A noun that names any person, place, or thing.

compare To decide how people and things are alike.

complex sentence A sentence with two parts, a simple sentence and a dependent clause.

compound sentence A sentence made up of two simple sentences joined by a conjunction.

conclusion A good guess about something the author does not say directly.

conjunction Joining words such as *and, or, but,* and *so.* Conjunctions appear after a comma in a compound sentence.

context Sentences or details that help explain a particular word or phrase.

contrast To decide how people and things are different.

D

dependent clause A group of words that does not express a complete thought. A dependent clause may be found in a complex sentence.

detail Facts and examples that give more information about the main idea.

diagram An illustration that shows important details, such as how something works. A diagram may have labels or captions to tell what its parts show.

dictionary A reference book that contains an alphabetical list of words along with their meanings, pronunciations, parts of speech, and other information.

dictionary entry A word and its definition listed in a dictionary or glossary.

digital dictionary A reference source available online or on portable disks that provides meanings for words.

directions Text that tells how to do something step by step.

domain The subject a text is about.

domain-specific vocabulary Words related to a specific topic, such as science.

drama A story written to be acted out.

E

effect An event that happens because of an earlier action.

evaluate To form an opinion about something.

exclamation A sentence that shows a strong feeling and ends with an exclamation point (!).

expository nonfiction Text that gives facts about what something is, how something works, or why something is important.

F

fable A short story in which a character, usually an animal that behaves like a person, learns a lesson.

fact Something that can be proved true.

fairy tale A kind of traditional tale with magical characters and events.

fantasy An imaginative story with characters or events that are not real.

feelings A person's emotions about something or someone.

folktale A story that has been told for many years. A folktale often has a moral, or lesson.

formal language A serious and polite form of speaking or writing.

future tense Verb form which describes a future action.

G

glossary A text feature found at the end of a book that provides an alphabetical listing of specialized words, their meanings, and other information.

graphic features Artwork, such as pictures, diagrams, and charts, that gives readers more information about the text.

H

heading Tells the reader what a section of text is about.

historical fiction A story that is set in the past and tells about things that could happen in a real time and place.

homograph A word that has the same spelling as another word but has a different meaning and may be pronounced differently.

homophone A word that sounds the same as another word but is spelled differently and has a different meaning.

humorous fiction Story that has characters and events that are funny. The setting and characters may be unrealistic.

I

idiom An expression with a special meaning different from the usual meanings of the individual words.

illustration Artwork that helps show a story's events.

imagery The use of vivid descriptions that help readers form an image, or picture, in their minds.

informal language A more relaxed form of speaking or writing.

informational text Text that gives factual information about a topic.

informative writing Writing that gives facts about a topic.

L

legend An old story that people have told for many years. The events of the story may or may not be true.

literal meaning The exact meaning of a word or phrase.

M

main idea The most important idea in a text.

map A drawing of an area, such as a neighborhood, town, or state.

message A story's lesson or moral.

monitor To check one's understanding.

mood The overall feeling of a story.

moral A lesson that is usually taught through something that happens to a main character or through what the character learns.

motivation The reason a character acts a certain way.

myth A story that tells what a group of people believe about the world.

N

....

narrative nonfiction A selection that gives information about a topic but is told as a story.

narrative writing Writing that tells a story. A narrative tells about something that happened to a person or a character.

nonliteral meaning The symbolic or figurative meaning of a word.

noun Names a person, a place, or a thing.

O

....

object pronoun A word that takes the place of the object: *me, you, him, her, it, us, them.* An object pronoun follows action verbs and words such as *to, for, at, of,* and *with.*

opinion Something that tells someone's thought, feeling, or belief.

opinion writing Writing that tells what the writer believes and gives reasons.

P

....

part of speech The way a word is used in a sentence, for example, noun, verb, or adjective.

past tense Verb form which describes a past action.

photograph Shows true pictures of important text details.

play A story that can be performed for an audience.

plot The problem that characters face and the events of the story.

plural noun A noun that names more than one person, place, or thing.

poetry Uses the sound and rhythm of words to show images and express feelings.

point of view How one thinks or feels about a subject.

possessive noun Shows that a person or animal owns or has something.

possessive pronoun Takes the place of a possessive noun to show who or what owns or has something.

precise words Words that are descriptive and exact.

predicate The action part of the sentence that tells what the subject does or did.

prefix A word part added to the beginning of a base word. A prefix changes the meaning of the base word but cannot stand alone.

present tense Verb form which describes action that happens in the present.

pronoun A word that takes the place of one or more nouns in a sentence.

proper noun A noun that names a particular person, place, or thing. A proper noun begins with a capital letter.

Q

....

question A type of sentence that asks something and ends with a question mark (?).

question To ask yourself questions about a selection before, during, and after reading.

quotation marks Punctuation marks (" ") that indicate dialogue. Quotation marks show the exact words a person says.

R

realistic fiction Story that has characters and events that are like those in real life.

research report Writing that tells what a writer learned from doing research about a topic.

rhyme When words end with the same sound. Rhyme is often found in poems.

run-on An error in which a writer joins two simple sentence without using a comma or a conjunction.

S

scene A section division of a play, similar to chapters in a book.

sequence The order in which different steps or events happen.

series When you list three or more words together in a sentence. Commas separate the words in a series.

series books Books that tell different stories about the same character.

setting Where and when a story takes place.

shades of meaning Slight differences in meaning among words that are related, especially words that describe degrees of certainty.

signal word A word that indicates a cause and its effect.

simple sentence A group of words that tells a complete thought. A simple sentence has a subject and a predicate.

singular noun A noun that names only one person, place, or thing.

stage directions Instructions to actors on how to move and speak.

stanza A group of lines in a poem. Stanzas often follow a rhyming pattern.

statement A type of sentence that tells something and ends with a period (.).

steps in a procedure Directions that are written in sequence.

story structure The characters, setting, and plot of a story.

subject The naming part of a sentence that tells *who* or *what*.

subject pronoun A word that takes the place of a subject: *I, you, he, she, it, we, they.*

subordinating conjunction Joins a dependent clause to the main part of a sentence. Some subordinating conjunctions are *because, after, when,* and *if.*

suffix A word part that is added to the end of a base word. A suffix changes the meaning of the base word but cannot stand alone.

summarize To briefly tell the important parts of a text in your own words.

synonym A word that has the same, or nearly the same, meaning as another word.

T

text and graphic features Sidebars, diagrams, and photographs outside of the main body of the text.

text features Parts of text, such as special type, speech balloons, and labels, that help readers find information.

theme An author's message about life to the reader.

thesaurus A book that provides a list of words, arranged in alphabetical order, and their synonyms.

timeline A line that shows the order in which events happened.

traditional tale A story that people have told for many years.

traits A person's qualities.

trickster tale An imaginative story in which one character tricks another.

V

verb The main word in the predicate.

visualize To create a mental picture.

W

word ending A word part, such as *-s, -ed,* or *-er,* added to the end of a base word.

word family A group of words with a common pattern, such as the same base word.

word root A word part from which other words are formed.